# REALISTIC LAYOUTS

## USE THE ART OF ILLUSION
## TO MODEL LIKE A PRO

CJ Riley

Kalmbach
Media

## Dedication

This book is dedicated to the long-gone and oft-lamented ICFS, the Iron City Ferroequinological Society of Pittsburgh. Both my modeling and my writing greatly benefited from our association, and it was through your friendship and considerable assistance that I developed my own "Sense of Rightness." So, to Tony, Larry, and Jim: "I'll take a cup of kindness yet, for Auld Lang Syne."
—CJ Riley

The Iron City Ferroeqinological Society, less one—Tony Thompson, Larry Kline, and CJ Riley—pose in front of three-truck Shay no. 4 of the Cass Scenic Railroad at Cass, W.Va., circa 1980. Missing is Jim Ruffing. We were much younger, but with much less wisdom in those long-ago halcyon days.

**On the cover:** Paul Dolkos modeled early spring in New England—the tree challenge had been solved with a mix of evergreens and scratch built bare branch trees. The effect is reinforced by the simple backdrop. Note also the road that curves behind the scenery, rather than being pushed against the backdrop. *Paul Dolkos*

**Facing page:** Weathering is an important part of creating realistic scenes. CJ Riley scratchbuilt Pochahontas Coal, aging the finish and weathering to make it look like an old, heavily used structure. *CJ Riley*

**Kalmbach Media**
21027 Crossroads Circle
Waukesha, Wisconsin 53186
www.KalmbachHobbyStore.com

Published in 2020
25  24  23  22  21    2  3  4  5  6

Manufactured in China

ISBN: 978-1-62700-771-9
EISBN: 978-1-62700-772-6

**Editor:** Jeff Wilson
**Book Design:** Lisa Bergman

Library of Congress Control Number: 2019952914

# Contents

# Foreword

If you take away only one concept from this thought-provoking book, I'll nominate this comment from chapter one: "But the one truism here is: The closer you adhere to prototype practices, the more the results are likely to have that 'sense of rightness.'"

Modelers do not start with the proverbial clean sheet of paper. We are, by definition, "modeling." That means we look to an actual object or even an action to emulate as well as our skills and other resources allow. The art of illusion comes in as we try to convince the viewer that something only a fraction of the "prototype's" size is a suitable stand-in for the original. As CJ implies, the farther we walk out on the limb called "freelancing," the more difficult it is to convince anyone that we aren't merely playing with nice toys.

Just as we start out with an obvious benchmark—the prototype—so too do our visitors bring with them a sense of what to expect. They may never have seen the Santa Fe in 1947 or the Nickel Plate Road in 1954 or even Conrail in 1995, but they do remember what Arizona or Indiana or Pennsylvania looked like at specific points in time. That is, they have an innate "sense of rightness" that they will automatically superimpose upon what we do as we attempt to build a model railroad—or, to put it more succinctly, a model of a railroad. Even the freelancer cannot escape the bounds of reality; the fabric of history can be stretched only so far before it rips apart.

Not everyone aspires to model railroading, as opposed to building interesting models of railroad hardware. Modeling railroading implies that we model not only the material objects employed by professional railroaders but also the actions they take to get cargo and people safely and efficiently from A to Z. Some of us are content to build nice models and run them around an oval of track, whereas others—including me—insist that the models perform every bit as realistically as they appear. I think of that as amortizing my considerable investment in thought, time, and money.

Taken to its ultimate potential, a model railroad is a time machine. My goal is to transport myself and my operating crew back to the mid-1950s when steam was making a valiant last stand against internal combustion. I was a newly minted teenager then, a bit naïve to the paradigm shift I was witnessing. But I have crystal-clear memories of that time and place, and I want to share them with others. I am therefore using the art of illusion in an attempt to convince the participants that they have important jobs to perform to ensure that the Nickel Plate's vaunted *High Speed Service* reputation remains intact at the end of each modeled—re-created, simulated—day.

CJ offers a host of opportunities for your consideration, various tools and techniques to use in your own quest to embrace the art of illusion to enhance the impact of your modeling endeavors. But keep foremost in mind the simple fact that you do not have a free hand here. You cannot hide behind the oft-heard mantra that "It's my railroad, and I can do anything I want!" No, you can't—not if your goal is to convince the viewer, not to mention yourself, that you've done a credible job of depicting a specific place and time.

To that end, this book represents an important tool in your arsenal. Use it wisely and be rewarded accordingly.

*Tony Koester*
*Newton, New Jersey*
*November 2019*

# Introduction

The lonesome wail of a steam whistle echoes off the steep, forested walls of a remote canyon of the Blackwater River deep in the heart of West Virginia. Soon the methodical asynchronous chuffing of two hard-working steam locomotives can be heard over the din of rushing water tumbling amongst the enormous boulders that clutter the nearby riverbed. A Western Maryland coal train appears around a bend, then curves along a concrete retaining wall and over a stone arch culvert, its thundering exhaust almost drowning out the clattering, banging and screeching of 60 loads of coal making their way upgrade.

This scene could have taken place in the heart of the Alleghenies in 1950, or it could have happened today in the basement of a skillful model railroader. The current offerings in rolling stock, scenery materials, and sound-equipped locomotives make a believably modeled scene such as this within the reach of most modelers.

This book is aimed at those folks whose goal is building a miniature transportation system, regardless of scale or available space. For them, the goal is an operating model railroad with realistic replicas of rolling stock moving through scenes that recall a time and place of their choosing. I will be

This June 1952 shot of a westbound Western Maryland freight at Frostburg, Md., led by one of the line's massive Decapods, provides an observation example. The ballast has a "razor" edge from an era when labor was cheap and the track crews took immense pride in the condition of their assigned section of track. Cinders cover the roadbed outside the ballast line. The adjacent track (normally uphill) shows a white film from traction sand that's been ground to a powder by locomotive wheels. Contaminants in the boiler water have stained the locomotive's drivers and air tank, and there are soot stains on the stack and dirt on the cylinder heads as well as the front air tank. *GC Corey photo, Herb Harwood collection*

"There is a little thing called 'imagination' which must play an important part on any model railroad."—*John Allen*

delighted if these folks learn from this material, understand the possibilities of going a step or two further than the simplified approaches advocated by many hobbyists, and adopt some of these suggestions.

It is for those who strive for that "sense of rightness" in capturing the flavor of the real world that I have written this book. I don't claim many of the ideas to be completely original, as I have been accumulating my knowledge through more than 50 years of National Model Railroad Association meets and conventions, along with informal bull sessions, magazine articles, and just plain looking out the windows of autos and passenger trains.

My education as an architect taught me to truly see and interpret what I was looking at, and to break large projects down to a series of small tasks. My basic process for this is the Observation/Understanding/Selection procedure, which works as follows:

OBSERVATION: We must carefully observe the real world. Without prototype railroads, their rights-of-way, associated structures, rolling stock, locomotives, and the country through which they run, we would be in a different hobby.

UNDERSTANDING: We must take the time to learn the *why* and *how* behind the observations. Why did the railroad curve around that hill instead of using a tunnel?

Why are the signals located where they are? Why is that depot painted in a different scheme than the others on that line? Why is there an earthen fill across a gully instead of a bridge or trestle?

SELECTION: We can't model everything, so it's important to select those observed items that are most important to a believable result, using the understanding previously discussed. For modelers, this often means "signature items"—the Baltimore & Ohio's color position light signals or the Southern Pacific's cab-forward steam locomotives, for example. There are other examples you'll find on your favorite railroad, town, or location.

Understand that my opinions—even if I state them in a "rule-like" way—are just opinions. Perhaps it is important for all of us to remember a very wise thing Tony Koester once said: "You may choose to do it that way, but I wouldn't." You may not agree with all of my summaries throughout this book, or have other preferences, but the basic ideas behind them are what I hope you take with you. I'm still learning, and I hope you all are too.

*CJ Riley*
*Port Hadlock, Washington*
*November 2019*

1

# Planning a realistic model railroad

**CSX SD50 8525 attacks the western slope of the Alleghenies, shoving an eastbound manifest freight under the Western Maryland's abandoned Keystone Viaduct in 2002. Note the subtle weathering on the locomotive and bridge, the dark rust color of the rail, the deep ballast, and the stone outcroppings along the cut.**
*Bill Metzger*

The magical "sense of rightness"—the ability to capture the feeling of a real railroad or scene, **1**—that we strive for begins in the planning stage of a model railroad. I'm not speaking of track design here, but the planning of what will become a miniature transportation system. While thinking at this level may seem "over the top" to novice or even intermediate modelers, these decisions can be critical to narrowing choices and defining a path leading to that goal of realism.

John Allen created a somewhat fantastic world "somewhere in the western mountains" with his famous HO scale Gorre & Daphetid. It was a land of steep grades, fanciful bridges, and wild, rocky countryside. While John was an avid student of prototype railroading, his undeniable first-rate modeling stretches the freelance category well toward the fantasy level. *John Allen; Peter Prunka collection*

The early morning mist often hangs heavy and cool along the river valleys in Appalachia. A Virginian & Ohio manifest freight passes a coal drag at Dawson Spring on W. Allen McClelland's seminal HO railroad. Allen was a pioneer in prototype freelancing and espoused the concept of "beyond the basement"— providing connections with other railroads, both prototype and model, so that cars could be interchanged and goods moved across the country. *W. Allen McClelland*

This early planning should begin with some clearly defined concepts. Some questions to ask:

• Is the projected railroad to be based on a specific prototype, freelanced based on a prototype, completely freelanced, or fantasy?

• If prototype based, what kind of traffic dominates?

• What's the overall railroad style? Is it a multi-track main line, secondary single-track, branch line, short line, industrial railroad, urban switching line, or something else?

• What's the era? Can it be narrowed to a specific year?

• What season do you want to represent?

## Prototype, freelance, or fantasy

Prototype or freelanced—there is no right or wrong here. Many modelers have been very successful in creating entirely fictitious worlds. The legendary John Allen's Gorre & Daphetid is a classic example of complete freelancing. His railroad was satisfying to himself and brought untold joy to several generations of modelers despite a very high level of fantasy. His only location parameter was "somewhere in the west" and he successfully combined dramatic chasms spanned by somewhat fanciful

Following the lead of the Chessie System, Allen joined the V&O with several other model railroads in that part of the world to create a quasi-merger—The Appalachian Lines— with the early paint modification illustrated on the lead Alco here climbing Sandy Summit grade. *W. Allen McClelland*

bridges with a bustling seaport. As he was a professional photographer, John's work was extensively published and widely viewed throughout the hobby press, and his modeling skills and advocacy of realistic weathering of rolling stock and structures greatly influenced the hobby, **2**.

John's work was typical of the era in which it was begun, the 1950s. In those days there wasn't the great variety of prototype locomotives we have today, and while the plastic rolling stock industry was just beginning, it was

considered prudent (and acceptable) to decorate every model for the most popular prototypes, whether those railroads owned those cars or not. If a modeler wanted to adhere to the practices of a prototype railroad, a great deal of scratchbuilding was required. For the next 30 years or so, freelancing was an obvious choice for most modelers.

Another modeling legend, Allen McClelland, rose to prominence in the 1970s, **3**, **4**. His Virginian & Ohio received similar publicity. It was more

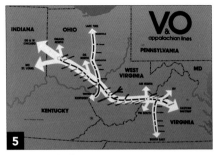

The Appalachian Lines connections to the V&O are shown on this map, firmly setting the railroads in a real location and providing connections to the outside world. *W. Allen McClelland*

than a layout—it was his creation of a complete transportation system, which included a route superimposed on a map of the region (Appalachia), interchanges with other railroads (model and prototype), and hidden staging tracks to represent "beyond the basement" trackage, **5**.

The V&O's carefully considered solid blue paint and simple lettering scheme was typical of the Appalachian railroads in Allen's chosen era: originally 1957, early diesels with some steam. The locomotives and rolling stock were carefully chosen to be appropriate for both that time and location. An operating system was devised that clearly indicated the modeled portion of the railroad was the easternmost division of an east-west railroad running from Afton, Va., to Dayton and Mansfield, Ohio.

Allen's concept was labeled "prototype freelancing"—meaning the railroad was fictitious, but it was very much rooted in the real world (down to the route drawn on a real map). Tony Koester, then editor of *Railroad Model Craftsman*, both promoted the concept and adopted it for his own Allegheny Midland, **6**. There were numerous prototypically freelanced railroads begun during that era, including my own Kanawha & Western Allegheny, **7, 8**.

I liked the freedom of prototype freelancing, but felt the need for modeling real places. My goal became adapting suitable real towns and track arrangements from Appalachia while changing names that did not appear on the route map. That melding of

Tony Koester was another early proponent of proto-freelancing. Sunrise, Va., was the southern terminus of his HO scale Allegheny Midland (Midland Road). This photo shows an AM coal drag entering Sunrise Yard as a transfer run from the Virginian & Ohio's nearby Santel Yard (behind F units, right) waits on the main before backing into the yard. The yard, tucked into a narrow valley below steep hillsides with the C&O-style tower, presents a clear image of its West Virginia location. *Tony Koester*

freelance and prototype provides some discipline while allowing considerable creativity. For example, the classic railroad town of Thurmond, W.Va., has been modeled, but renamed Armstrong, in honor of both John Armstrong (the revered track planner) and a family name given to my eldest son.

The computer revolution enabled more complicated custom die work, and by the 2000s, locomotive models detailed correctly for specific railroads became both readily available and affordable. Methods such 3-D printing, silicone rubber molds, resin casting and laser cutting allowed for low-

**7** My own Kanawha & Western Allegheny was heavily influenced by Allen and Tony. Here, a K&WA 2-8-0 with loaded hoppers thunders down "the main street" of Armstrong, W.Va., a model of real-life Thurmond. Thurmond faces the C&O main line along the New River. This is a case of prototype-freelancing a railroad, but modeling a real town and track plan. *CJ Riley*

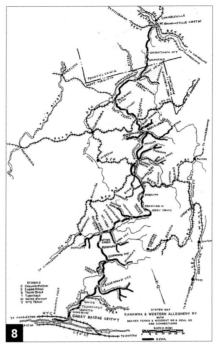

**8** This map, following the style of the B&O's subdivision maps, illustrates the Kanawha's route through West Virginia into Pennsylvania. It sets my model railroad in the real world, providing appropriate connections and interchanges and a rational basis for modeling decisions. *CJ Riley*

volume production of very accurate and prototype specific rolling stock and structures.

Today it is possible and quite practical to assemble a roster of locomotives and rolling stock that are accurate for a great many major (and secondary) railroads, without resorting to expensive limited-run, imported brass models. The phenomenal growth and resources of railroad historical societies, combined with the internet explosion, makes prototype research much more feasible for the average modeler. These factors have made the concept of accurate modeling of a specific prototype more appealing to many, and there has been a growing interest in modeling a specific portion of a prototype line.

An example is Tony Koester, who abandoned the Nickel Plate-influenced Allegheny Midland for a careful re-creation of a portion of the Nickel Plate's high-speed Midwest raceway. Jack Burgess is well known for his careful rendition of the Yosemite Valley Railroad in August 1939. Jack models locomotives, structures, and scenery from his extensive collection of historic photographs, taking care that the figures and even piles of junk are modeled as they appear in the photos, **9**. His book *Trains to Yosemite* is a comprehensive treatment of that railroad.

It is hard to argue against the excitement and appeal of accurate equipment running through a readily recognized prototype scene in any scale. When one adds the capabilities of Digital Command Control (DCC) and sound systems that even include the proper whistle or horn tones for various locomotives, the appeal of prototype modeling is hard to resist.

The opposite end of the spectrum would be a high level of fantasy. This approach appeals to many, and as mentioned earlier, despite a high interest in the prototype, John Allen endowed his Gorre & Daphetid with a very high fantasy component. Fantasy modeling allows one to create exaggerated landscapes and spindly bridges only remotely based on reality. These railroads often take on a mining or logging theme, portraying dinky locomotives and tiny cars, often riding on extremely narrow gauge rails with similarly undersized structures with lots of "cutesy" appeal. This approach often attracts those who like to scratchbuild or kitbash equipment and structures, and they enjoy the freedom to create their own designs, no matter how remote from the real world.

An excellent example of this approach is Greg Wright's Republic

**9** Strict prototype modeling has become the choice of many. Jack Burgess faithfully models the Yosemite Valley RR in August 1939 in HO scale. Here is the turntable at El Portal with the prototype scene (right) and Jack's models. *Jack Burgess*

**10**

Greg Wright chose a mining theme for his large-scale narrow gauge layout. Here a 1:28 scale narrow gauge Shay trundles among the mill buildings with a train of diminutive rolling stock. *Greg Wright*

Mining Co., a wonderful G scale (large-scale narrow gauge) railroad in a relatively small space with slight exaggeration of the elements, **10**. The tiny locos shuttle about the massive installation of the Republic Mining Co., where the buildings tower up to the ceiling but are very shallow. This is the essence of, for want of a better term, fantasy modeling

There you have it! Your first major decision, although your final choice can be one you slowly gravitate toward after trying several possibilities. None of your other decisions, save only scale, will have such impact on your railroad's ultimate personality. But the one truism here is: the closer you adhere

to prototype practices, the more the results are likely to have that "sense of rightness." Thus, whatever your choice, if you are not going to model a specific prototype, it's a distinct advantage to model "from the prototype." Learning about prototype railroads can help tremendously with decision making down the road. Why invent everything when the prototype has done much of the work for you?

## Choosing a region

Even if you've made the decision to model a specific railroad—let's say the Santa Fe—there are still myriad choices. Do you model the Chicago metro area, the plains of Kansas, the

deserts of New Mexico or Arizona, the climb through Cajon Pass, or the Surf line between San Diego and Los Angeles? Equipment and scenery differ greatly among these regions. Similar variations exist with virtually any prototype.

The point here is that a sense of believability begins with a commitment to, and understanding of, a location, be it local or regional. There are many subtle clues, other than the lettering on railroad rolling stock. Nothing says New England quite like a covered bridge, even though they were more common in other regions. Barns differ: a typical Appalachian barn, **11**, will differ in appearance from one in New England, **12**, the Midwest, or California. There will be other such subtleties to be studied and understood. Whether you are freelancing or modeling a prototype, choosing a region and learning about it is key to providing viewers the feeling that they have been there, seen photos, or otherwise recognize your intentions. After that, it's a matter of creating a representation with some level of accuracy.

## Traffic

A few decades ago, before the number of Class 1 roads was severely reduced by the merger mania that began in the 1960s, most railroads could be identified with a few dominant commodities: lumber products from the Northwest, coal in Appalachia, **13**, grain and cattle on the Plains, and fruit from California and Florida. While coal, timber and farm products are still common on the rails, many modern railroads seem to be dominated by container traffic—imported products being moved from coastal ports and empties being returned (with some loads) for export.

While most major railroads carried a variety of products, often hidden in boxcars or reefers, it was frequently the open cars (flats, gondolas, and hoppers) that clearly set a theme for recognizable traffic. The Pittsburgh & Lake Erie, a New York Central subsidiary, was a classic example. As a line serving the steel industry that dominated the valleys of the

**11**

Split-rail snake fences are a signature item on Appalachian farms, as are the roughly split wood shake roofs and unpainted walls of this raised barn. *CJ Riley*

**12**

A classic red barn, stone fences, and the white farmhouse with its jumble of additions are a strong image of New England. The background barn and house were modeled in N scale (1:160) to create a forced perspective on Paul Dolkos' HO railroad. *Paul Dolkos*

**13**

Open loads make railroad-carried commodities easy to identify, such as these Norfolk & Western hoppers filled with coal. Take note of details such as the wig-wag signal, the white church on the hill, and the way the haze softens the colors in the background. *Larry Kline*

Monongahela and Ohio rivers in Pennsylvania, incoming loads of ore, coal, coke, limestone and other needed commodities in hopper cars, along with outgoing loads of coiled steel, pipe, castings, and machinery loaded on flats and gondolas made for a profitable railroad. The line also carried considerable east/west bridge traffic in house cars (enclosed cars such as boxcars and reefers) as goods moved east and west through interchanges with other lines at the Youngstown, Ohio and Connellsville, Pa., connections. Although that would seem a good mix of traffic, the P&LE ultimately withered with the steel industry, finally dying as mergers killed off the road's bridge traffic.

Many other regions were similarly dominated by single commodities or industries. One of the exceptions to open cars defining traffic might be a solid train of reefers rolling eastbound in the West, clearly indicating California farm produce. Similarly, strings of boxcars (in early eras) or more modern covered hoppers portray grain traffic, and strings of stockcars or meat reefers likewise define traffic.

Once again, while decisions on prototype and location help to define traffic, further decisions regarding visual characteristics, era, and even season impact traffic, and therefore rolling stock and operations.

## Characteristics

Whether based on a stretch of a prototype railroad, freelanced, or fantasy, the question of characteristics or style of the railroad must be accounted

for. The Pennsy's four-track main line around Horseshoe Curve, **14**, means signals, heavy rail and highly maintained roadbed, an almost constant parade of trains, and other

**14**

Pennsylvania Railroad's Horseshoe Curve, one of the country's most iconic railroad locations, was rarely still, and multiple-train meets were common on its four well-maintained tracks. Here two passenger trains meet in a 1950s scene.
*Trains magazine collection*

15

Branch and secondary lines in the plains states featured wheat and corn fields, grain elevators, and lots of boxcars. This scene is at Bayneville, Kan., in late summer 1952. *Jeff Wilson collection*

16

Paul Dolkos' new HO layout has embraced urban railroading. It's April in Baltimore, and the beer delivery guys are swapping tales as they deliver their wares to Pappas Liquors in Highlandtown. The rowhouse facades are signature Baltimore icons that are recognizable to those who know the area. The facades in the background are photos from the area pasted onto poster board. *Paul Dolkos*

characteristics typical of first-class mainline railroading.

A granger branch line wandering through wheat fields to small towns and their grain elevators implies very different characteristics, **15**. A backwoods logging line with rough ties, no ballast, big trees, and rough wooden structures is different still. Railroading in the urban canyons of Chicago or Baltimore means small locomotives, street running, and lots of switching, **16**. Choosing the character of a railroad impacts choice of prototype, equipment, track design, scenery, and operational style.

## Era

Choice of era impacts all other choices. Over and above the implications of steam or diesel power, era affects appropriate freight and passenger car styles as well as the newest locomotive designs that can appear. Does your era have wooden, open-vestibule, heavyweight, lightweight streamlined, or Amtrak passenger cars? Truss rod, USRA, or all-steel freight cars? Double-stack well cars and containers? Naturally, there is much overlap as equipment had a life span of several decades, but a mix appropriate for the chosen era is critical to believability.

Era also impacts the right-of-way and industrial buildings. Up into the 1950s, labor was relatively cheap and section gangs were numerous, generally being responsible for regular inspection and grooming of short sections of main line, perhaps 6 miles. Examination of photos from the '40s and '50s show incredible attention to maintaining the right-of-way in almost park-like condition. Ballast lines were constantly touched up with rakes, leaving a crisp clean edge. Buildings were well maintained and regularly painted.

Such was not the case by the 1970s. Machines were used to clean ballast and adjust track work, spreading ballast across the roadbed. Depots, often no longer needed, were boarded up or demolished. Interlocking towers were abandoned, replaced by modern signaling systems, distant dispatchers and radios.

17

Depicting a season can have an operational as well as visual impact, as traffic levels often change with the seasons. Paul Dolkos modeled early spring in New England—the tree challenge was solved with a mix of evergreens and scratchbuilt bare-branch trees. The effect is reinforced by the simple backdrop. Note also the road that curves behind the scenery, rather than being pushed against the backdrop. *Paul Dolkos*

**LEARNING POINTS**

**1.** Choose a prototype and region to model.

**2.** Decide on the level of prototype fidelity desired.

**3.** Be specific about era, location, and season.

**4.** Learn about traffic patterns and characteristics of your prototype.

**5.** Don't be afraid to wander down a few side tracks.

**Paul Dolkos created a temporary winter scene by applying marble dust (later vacuumed up) to what had been a spring scene. There's no reason such a scene couldn't be permanent.** *Paul Dolkos*

Modeling a specific era focuses research efforts. There is nothing wrong with trying to learn everything about the Union Pacific, but there's almost 150 years of history to learn. It is much easier to learn everything about the UP on Sherman Hill in the 1950s, and a lot about the rest of the story.

## Season

Choice of season obviously has an immediate impact on scenery, but it can also impact equipment, operations, and details, **17, 18**. Many lines have seasonal traffic increases. Grain or potato harvests mean a fall rush in traffic, as do many west coast fruits and vegetables, while southern produce may have a different harvest time. Iron ore shipments from the Mesabi by boat through the Great Lakes are suspended for winter ice, ending the long trains of hoppers loaded with ore southbound for the steel mills of Pittsburgh. Heating coal shipments pick up in late summer, then taper off in spring.

Passenger traffic also has seasonal patterns. Fall and winter mean a sizable increase in passenger travel from New York and Chicago heading south for warmer climes, often resulting in longer trains (or additional trains as extras or second sections) and often use equipment from other roads where this season is slower. There are football specials, ski trains, summer trains to northern cottages, and I'm sure research on your chosen area will reveal other patterns.

## Putting it together

Where does all this planning lead? If the era, season, location and equipment are all appropriate and consistent, then creating the proper illusion needs only appropriate structures and scenery. However, the reverse is also true: If there's a mixture of equipment and paint schemes that were not found together on the prototype, or there is inconsistency in the setting, then it takes a great leap of faith by an observer to accept what he or she sees. It won't feel right, or appear realistic, to anyone but the builder.

As a final word, don't feel that this tight commitment is always necessary, particularly for a newer modeler. If you haven't locked in these decisions, then take some time to explore alternatives. Remember the old bumper sticker: Just because I'm wandering, it doesn't mean I'm lost!

# CHAPTER TWO

# Secrets to life-like backdrops

Appropriate backdrops can be created for any terrain. Here, a Chessie Steam Special headed by Chesapeake & Ohio no. 614 cruises through the rolling farmland of Washington County, Pa., between Pittsburgh and Wheeling, W.Va. The key to turning this into a backdrop (painted or photographic) is the embankment tree and shrubbery lines along both sides of the track that would screen the joint between scenery and backdrop. *CJ Riley*

In visiting a tremendous number of model railroads over the past 50 years, I have concluded that a missing backdrop may be the biggest illusion buster of all. Prototype scenes are enhanced by their backgrounds, whether it be rolling hills, **1**, or walls of factory buildings. Thus, I find there is nothing more distracting than a concrete-block wall and its grid of mortar joints hovering over beautiful scenery and structures.

The good news is that we have several options open to us for creating realistic backdrops, from a simple sky background to rolling hills to detailed structures. The first step, though, is planning—preferably before construction (or at least before scenery is installed). By planning and beginning the backdrop early in the construction of a layout, **2**, it's much easier to attach furring strips or build a stud wall (or whatever else is needed) to hide things that shouldn't be part of a believable scene *before* something breakable is installed in front of it.

Since most backdrop materials come in rolls or large, cumbersome sheets, it's much easier to install them before any major construction is done. Yes, it is possible to reach across benchwork if there are no fragile structures or scenery to snag and damage, but it's much better to avoid the difficulty. I also recommend getting help with installing the base material; this is a classic case where four hands (or more) is far better than two.

## Backdrop materials

There are many appropriate background surfaces, and all will work well, *if* they are smooth and paintable. I have seen (or used) most of them:

drywall (gypsum or plaster board), aluminum coil stock, linoleum (the smooth back side), tempered hardboard (such as Masonite), and sheet styrene. I'm sure there are other possibilities, and there is no reason not to use several materials on one layout. I have used small lengths of linoleum to cove inside and outside corners, for example, on walls that were otherwise covered with rigid material.

Coving corners, or creating a curved surface, is a major plus when aiming for a believable backdrop. Hard corners create impossible-to-hide shadows and distortions in what should appear as a smooth summer sky or verdant hills. Ideally, coving is done in a smooth curve with the joints blended. If a situation precludes permanent attachment of coving material, it might be possible to use a short length of flexible material, such as styrene, taping it in place and painting over the tape. While the tape texture might still be slightly visible, the scene will be improved.

There may be situations where a smoothly curved cove is not possible. I have solved such a problem with a narrow strip of drywall or stiff cardstock placed at a 45-degree angle across the corner. Smoothing the joints with drywall compound or using paintable caulk blends the transition

**2**

**The Puget Sound Model Railroad Engineers model the railroads around Tacoma, Wash., along with the Northern Pacific line climbing to Stampede Pass. Mt. Rainier looms prominently on the horizon throughout the region, thus this image was a requirement on the backdrop for the upper deck. Painting before the upper-deck benchwork was in place simplified the process.** *CJ Riley*

**3** The detailed trestle in the foreground attracts the eye, reducing the importance of the impressionistic backdrop. Note how successive hills fade, adding depth to the scene. *CJ Riley*

and lessens most of the visual problems generated by a 90-degree corner.

Some go so far as to cove the wall to the ceiling, so that the sky continues overhead. The only real advantage from my point of view is for low-angle photographs that show a great deal of sky. If a lighting valance is used, little of the ceiling is in normal view, reducing the advantage of the cove. There is also the lessened light

reflection disadvantage if the ceiling is painted blue, and a layout needs as much light as possible.

## Finished appearance

Try to remember, the backdrops are just character actors and the stage, not the stars, so try to make the backdrop truly in the background and not an attention grabber, **3**. Let the trains, scenery, and structures stand out and be

the featured players.

The challenge for many modelers is creating the needed backdrop images. There are many possibilities: Commercial photo murals are available, or you can take and edit your own photos and have them printed on conventional photo prints, posters, or long continuous rolls. There also commercial printed backdrops that are not photos, but painted illustrations.

**4** Sketching and painting directly from a photograph simplifies the challenge and can make for a more realistic scene. It's not as difficult as it looks—give it a try! *CJ Riley*

**5** More mountainous terrain presents different challenges. This prototype scene makes it is easy to see how the detail lessens and the color fades with distance until the farthest ridge is a simple-to-paint blue-gray. *CJ Riley*

6

Otis McGee's Southern Pacific Shasta Division is set in northern California. This scene at Cantera Loop works well because of the depth. The painted farm buildings are far enough back to avoid the strange perspectives commonly seen with backdrop structures, and the modeled stream seems to continue up the painted valley. A modest improvement might be gained if the color in the painted stream was adjusted to more closely match that of the resin. *CJ Riley*

An artist can be commissioned for a custom paint job, or you can paint it yourself—and don't dismiss this possibility too quickly, **4**. Even a plain blue sky is a great improvement over a concrete wall, and distant natural features such as ridges or mountains quickly become a hazy blue-gray, **5**, which can be easy to paint. At worst, if you attempt to paint some background hills and they don't turn out, you can simply repaint the backdrop blue and try again.

## Painted backdrops
You have a great deal of leeway here, **6**. Simple jagged fir and hemlock tree lines on the ridges of the Northwest mountains, hazy blue-gray ridges of Appalachia, or the rolling yellow grass hills of coastal California, **7**, are all easily implied with simple painting techniques. If you're more ambitious, adopting a regional painting style

7

The burnt yellow grass hills of coastal California, interspersed with clusters of green live oaks, have their own characteristics that are clearly recognized. *CJ Riley*

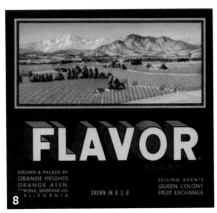

**Fruit crate labels can be an inspiration for backdrop painting. Their simplified style lends itself to an effective backdrop—California in this case. The very basic shapes and colors of the distant mountains are straightforward.** *CJ Riley collection*

might be appropriate. I have always thought that a California-themed backdrop done in the simplified style of old-time fruit-crate labels, **8**, or the style of one of the many regional painters would be wonderful. I am sure there are equivalent regional styles that could be adapted for other areas.

Even a simple blue sky works. If clouds are a must, wispy streams are easier than puffs of clouds. The puffs that occasionally march across the sky require an understanding of perspective that is best avoided. I have learned over the years that a bank of clouds looming over the horizon is much easier to paint, and can imply an approaching storm.

Remember, clouds are not pure white! Depending on the light, they may have a pink, yellow, or blue shade, and the underside is usually a slight blue-gray shadow. Like everything else, don't imagine a cloud when painting it—have a photo of the intended effect nearby for reference. If you must have clouds across the sky, there are stencils available that ease the chore.

When painting a backdrop, I've found it easiest to avoid including structures. It's difficult to pull off the perspective and detail and unnecessary. Painting a farm pasture is straightforward, and if needed it's simple to glue a cut-out photo of a barn looming over the shoulder of a hill. Include a tree, perhaps, or some low shrubbery to set the barn into the scene and you have included a farm by inference. A town could be implied with a few cut outs partially hidden in the backdrop, **9**. If doing this, I recommend a very light wash of gray to simulate distance and sealing the paper with matte medium to avoid moisture problems.

I maintain a file of potential backdrop photos. Many regional magazines, such as *Yankee* or *Arizona Highways,* contain potential background material relevant to the area being modeled. Don't be too restrictive, though, since a white frame church in New England could also be appropriate in West Virginia or Iowa. Small flaws or era incongruities, such as a modern logo on a sign, can be screened with a painted tree, for example, or covered with a more era- (or region-) appropriate sign.

Don't ignore images from paintings. A Norman Rockwell barn might be even better than a photo. If employing a regional style, paintings of appropriate structures found in that style would be a boon.

Modern scanners and photocopiers

**Larry Kline produced a viable, realistic backdrop starting with a basic sky and painted distant ridge line combined with a commercial backdrop that has had its sky removed. The small gap behind the actual scenery effectively implies distance across a valley.** *Larry Kline*

A professionally painted backdrop can offer much detail. The slight rise in the scenery, the row of trees, and the structures screen the transition from flat to 3-D on J.J. Johnson's railroad. *CJ Riley*

make collecting potential images from books or the internet that much easier, and they can be properly scaled before use.

Whatever method used for backdrop scenery, the realism is greatly improved if there is a separation, physical and/or visual, between scenery and backdrop. If the scenery rises even slightly as it approaches the backdrop and there is a gap of an inch or more to an apparently distant scene, then it will appear that the 3-dimensional scenery falls away down into a gully or valley before rising as an image on the backdrop.

This visual and physical separation is important to the illusion, no matter the components, **10**. Other visual separation tricks could include a fence line, an area of low shrubbery, piles of railroad ties or hay bales, even a cluster of small buildings. As you can see, almost anything that separates the joint between three-dimensional scenery and the backdrop will both improve the illusion and provide that old magician's trick—distraction. Any item that attracts the viewers eye causes

the backdrop to recede from both mind and view.

## Photo backdrops

For many years I questioned the value of photo-realistic backdrops, but I have

mellowed considerably, having seen some outstanding examples, **11**. The advent of digital cameras and image-editing software such as Photoshop makes photo use much more practical, particularly when used in short

This photo transformed my initial reluctance to embrace photo backdrops. The scene, on Tony Koester's HO circa-1954 Nickel Plate Road layout, uses a backdrop from a 35mm slide he took at this location back in the late 1960s. Tony scanned the photo, retouched it using Photoshop Elements, and had it printed on 18"-wide continuous-roll paper at a local graphics store. Note how the modeled road disappears around the hill before reappearing in the photo. More work on the crops and ground cover in this scene remains to be done. *Tony Koester*

# PHOTO-EDITING SOFTWARE

**The emergence of Photoshop** and other photo-editing software has revolutionized methods of making realistic backdrops. With the ever-growing focus on prototypical operations and the modeling of a portion of a favorite railroad, newer cutting-edge layouts are often multiple levels of very narrow benchwork, sometimes as little as a foot wide (or even shallower). That minimizes the scenery possibilities, so the backdrop often becomes the scenery, particularly when modeling "flatland" prototypes.

Tony Koester has adopted that approach for his late-1950s era Nickel Plate Road St. Louis Division layout (you can see one example in photo 13). He has made extensive use of photos taken along the prototype line to use in his backdrops, but photographs taken in the 1980s and '90s often show vast differences from his modeled era of the late 1950s. Here is how Tony captured one such scene and backdated it.—*CJ Riley*

**These images of the photo backdrop** at Veedersburg, Ind., on my HO scale Nickel Plate Road layout show the opportunities that we have today, thanks to the wide availability of photo-editing software. I use Photoshop Elements, which is inexpensive and quite powerful.

A narrow shelf design is no longer really seen as optional for those of us who see operation as the main goal, as mainline length becomes a major factor. This means we must find ways to extend the apparent depth of backdrops without actually modeling anything, so photo backdrops become critical. I now regard Elements and a computer as critical modeling tools—every bit as important as, say, an X-acto knife and glue.

I needed to model the junction at Veedersburg where the Peoria & Eastern (part of the New York Central System) crossed the Nickel Plate at grade. Other than the crossing itself, a short length of track on the layout, and the interlocking tower, the P&E would have to be represented on the backdrop—the entire scene measures just 16" deep from fascia to backdrop.

The photos show how I had to use a recent photo of Veedersburg taken after the Peoria & Eastern tracks had been pulled up. The depot was still standing, but almost devoid of paint, as was the grain elevator. By cloning the paint and using two other images of track for the main line and various sidings, changing the track detail (ballast, etc., using the Rubber Stamp or Clone tool) and the perspective (Skew tool), I was able to combine the images into one backdrop photo. The captions with the individual photos provide a general guideline of how I went through the process. I also airbrushed the entire image (using the Paintbrush tool set on a low percentage of opacity) when it was complete to dull the colors back to the sooty steam era.—*Tony Koester*

The finished scene illustrates how much realism can be created on a narrow shelf by using a photographic backdrop. Without the manipulated photo, there would be nothing but a blank wall or blue sky immediately behind the modeled **tower.** *Five photos: Tony Koester*

1. Here's the original image with some sky retouching started (to get rid of overhead electric lines). Note the rusted elevator and poor paint on the depot.

2. This is the former Nickel Plate main at Metcalf, Ill., which I reused for the P&E main at Veedersburg by erasing the surrounding terrain, making it look better maintained, and skewing the perspective.

3. A photo of the siding at Metcalf, Ill., provided the spur track for the orange grain elevator by erasing the surrounding terrain and skewing it to the desired perspective.

4. Here's how the backdrop photo looked before the track was finally aligned and ballasted and the diamond crossing finished. I wound up cutting out the photo along the tree line and gluing it to the sky-painted backdrop.

White wood-framed churches with tall steeples are signature structures in New England. This scene reinforces that sense of place between the modeled church and its neighbor on the photographic backdrop. The modeled graveyard surrounded with a hedge, combined with the row of bare trees, soften the backdrop transition. The bridge leads the road toward the backdrop but resolves the transition from scenery to backdrop with a sharp left turn. *Paul Dolkos*

stretches and combined with modeled or painted areas, **12**.

The technique has to be done well to be effective. Think about it this way: you want the focus to be on the trains first, then the surrounding structures, followed by scenery and finally the backdrop. If the backdrop is too well-detailed and sharp, it will draw too much attention to itself.

I have seen well-done photo backdrops, particularly when it is a city scene and appropriate photos from the area and era being modeled are used. This is especially effective when there is an iconic building depicted, one that many (perhaps most) people would recognize. But be careful of

perspectives that are out-of-whack with the modeling—this can call negative attention to the backdrop.

The illusion is compromised when a photo backdrop is from an area not modeled. As an example, I once visited a layout depicting Seattle that used a photo of downtown effectively behind the waterfront scene. It clearly was Seattle. But around a corner, where the backdrop was purportedly a different Seattle neighborhood, the builder had used a commercially available photo backdrop of the Pittsburgh riverfront. I was somewhat jarred by the recognition of my former hometown and even more startled when I was able to identify my former office window. The other folks in the room had no reaction to this, even though they were all from Seattle. Perhaps the overall high quality of the modeling overcame this anomaly, or perhaps this is evidence of the diminished importance of an accurate photo backdrop.

On the other hand, photos can be more challenging in backdrops when Mother Nature is the subject. It takes skill to properly match foreground scenery materials to the colors and textures in the backdrop. If there are modeled trees close to the backdrop, any less-than-perfect foliage representations, or even carefully crafted species-specific trees, will

Two rows of Busch plastic corn have been placed in front of a commercial cornfield backdrop on Tony Koester's NKP layout, although Tony says the backdrop looked better without the added corn. Again, the raised right of way typical of the Midwest screens the joint and provides some separation on this very narrow shelf benchwork. *Tony Koester*

normally pale by comparison to nearby tree photos—and that discrepancy will attract unwanted attention. This challenge can be minimized if the backdrop is of a distant scene with little up-close foliage or Midwest farmland, for example, **13**, or if most of the photographed trees are screened.

I've seen successful instances of early spring being depicted, where the bare-stick trees modeled are easy to blend into the bare trees in the photo backdrop. What helped was that there was no real color discrepancy among the mostly gray and black shades of both.

Nature photos seem to work better when the layout shelf is so narrow that there is insufficient space for significant scenery. This essentially makes the backdrop the scenery, so less comparison between nearby real and artificial items is possible. In these cases, a fenceline or some other break that screens the inevitable transition joint (such as the cornfield in **13**) will add greatly to the realism. A photo positioned between two modeled structures is also effective.

If a photo backdrop is used, consider having it slightly overexposed, or gray it down with a wash or light overspray. Dulling the colors will help the photo images fade into the distance. Don't forget that the effect of moisture or pollutants in the atmosphere (haze) fades the sharpness of distant objects. That haze does not usually occur in train rooms so it must be simulated.

**14**

**Tom Johnson is an art teacher and has the skills to make this road illusion work. I cannot locate the transition between scenery and photo backdrop in this scene. Skillful treatment of perspective and color, along with a fillet at the right-angle junction, make this HO scale northern Indiana scene work. The structures screen the scene from off-center viewing.** *Tom Johnson*

This is one of the best arguments for painting an impressionistic backdrop over photorealism.

## Backdrops and roads

One of the most common errors on model railroads is having a road running directly into the backdrop and stopping at the vertical wall or proceeding too far up it. Slight variations in color and perspective can quickly destroy the illusion, even if there is a smoothly coved transition between horizontal and vertical surfaces. Perspective that is perfectly rendered when viewed from the front may not look right when viewed

from either side. This problem can be mitigated if structures or trees on each side of the road screen the view from anywhere but directly in front, **14**.

If at all possible, try to avoid roads that run directly into the backdrop. One trick is to try to make roads run at an angle (or curve) and disappear behind a building or a grove of trees, then appear on the backdrop. If circumstances require a more direct road approach, letting the road rise slightly and then go down out of sight only to reappear as a painted road further off is an illusion that is both easier and more realistic than attempting a more direct approach.

**15**

**Tony Koester used photos he took in Metcalf, Ill. in this under-construction view that shows how he aligns the modeled roads with the backdrop. SceniKing tree backdrops will fill gaps between the photos. The sky has been trimmed off the original photos, which have been backdated by removing modern vehicles and details. The joint is screened somewhat by the buildings, but again, at the "off angle" there appears to be a bend.** *Tony Koester*

**16**

The transition from backdrop to modeled scenery is screened by structure flats, which are photos of buildings mounted on stiff cardstock in this unfinished scene. The flats work because the sides and roofs are not visible. *CJ Riley*

**17**

The "flat" flat problem can be resolved by angling the proposed flat so there's at least one side wall as in this warehouse building. A kit was simply unfolded, using the back wall to create a second wing—the back wall is now plain styrene. Textured brick sheet was inserted in the rear wing to make it taller, with the wall sign helping to disguise the splice joint. Note the corrugated metal addition stops at the roof ridge, since the rear slope is not normally visible. The other buildings are magazine picture cutouts pasted to the backdrop and blended in with painted trees. *CJ Riley*

Angling a road into a backdrop, **15**, can make it easier to use neighboring trees or structures to hide the joint. A viewer won't be able to see the backdrop joint from straight on, and even though it will still be visible from some angles, viewers will have to work harder to see it.

Using the principle of distraction can also help. A vehicle or two disrupting the view, such as a tractor-trailer blocking the road while backing into an alley, works well, as does an overhead bridge. Keep in mind that the higher the benchwork of the layout, the easier it is to create these illusions. An illusion can quickly fail if one can look over or around the distracting element.

## Building flats

Building flats can be effective if used properly, **16**, but if applied haphazardly or casually they can spoil the illusion of a scene. Flats can be very useful in tight spaces, but they need to be positioned well. A row of low building fronts with no roofs or side walls immediately jumps out (especially if

## LEARNING POINTS →

1. A backdrop is vital—even if it's just a sky blue background.

2. The backdrop is the stage, not an actor.

3. On a narrow shelf layout, a photo backdrop can serve as the scenery.

4. Shadows or inappropriate images can be painted out.

5. Large structure flats and low-relief buildings can serve as backdrops.

6. Steep and tall scenic items can work as flats.

7. Color-coordinating 3-D scenery and the backdrop is critical.

viewers are looking down at a scene). A much better illusion results if the flats are not truly "flat," but instead "low relief" and set at an angle to the backdrop, **17**.

A missing wall isn't a problem if it is around the corner from the viewer and there is a short visible wall on the exposed side as well as a piece of roof. Yes, a flat roof will be triangular, but invisible if the building is tall enough. If the roof is visible, a rooftop sign or carefully placed details such as HVAC equipment or large vents can conceal that problem, **18**. Likewise, short side walls combined with trees, fences, billboards, or other distractions that minimize the short-wall exposure will also work. If a low-relief building has a sloping roof, running the ridge along the backdrop allows the visible part of the roof to be modeled effectively.

Large structures with massive side walls, such as warehouses or large manufacturing plants, are ideal low-relief structures. These can usually be tall enough to hide a flat roof and there is ample opportunity for vents, piping, blowers and other appropriate details, both on the wall and the roof, to attract the eye and distract viewers from the appearance of a flat.

Don't restrict thinking to structure flats. Steep ridges or other almost vertical scenic features can also work well as flats and be used much like buildings. As you can see, there are myriad ways to create an effective backdrop. The advantages and disadvantages of each technique are many; you need to determine what is best for your layout and skills. Just make the most of the advantages and minimize the disadvantages using screening and distraction for a proper background for the real stars: the trains.

**18**

**Large industrial structures can serve as the primary backdrop. Here on Allen McClelland's Virginian & Ohio there's a bonus in that the building and a large tree help screen a track emerging through the backdrop from staging.** *W. Allen McClelland*

# CHAPTER THREE

# Planning realistic scenery

For most model railroaders, the vision of finished scenery—majestic mountains, **1**, rolling plains, golden hillsides, verdant forests, or a rugged and rocky coastline—is in the forefront of their minds from the initial layout concept. This is good, but many other decisions must be made and chores completed before work on this defining phase can begin.

**The New River winds through the deep gorge it has carved between the verdant hills in a wonderful example of Appalachian scenery and how isolated a mountain community can be. Note how the CSX freight is dwarfed by the scenery as it crosses the river from the Dunloup Creek branch and rumbles into Thurmond, W.Va. This is a great illustration of the "angle of repose" of soil. The slope of the ridges is about 30 degrees, pretty much the standard natural slope, though a rocky hill can be steeper. Model hillsides could be up to 45 degrees and still look fine; steeper if observed only face on. Note the texture of the foliage and how, although autumn color is in its early stages, there is variation in the shades of green.** *Kevin Scanlon*

**2**

Scenery planning involves leaving enough room for all elements. Here, although the bridge is properly skewed and there is some terrific texture in the earthen "embankment," the vertical wall of soil in the foreground is a realism killer that is all too often seen. It would have been better to use a retaining wall or make the slope of earth lean back closer to the mine spurs, deleting the abandoned track. *CJ Riley*

**3**

This photo shows a highway, but the grading is very similar to that of a railroad grade. Note that the hillside is not a simple slope, but has many humps and depressions, with obvious erosion patterns. The cut at left clearly shows how the roadbed is notched into the hill and at upper center has a bank on both sides as it passes through a shoulder. There's obvious fill in the low spots, including rock to deter erosion. *CJ Riley*

While the actual scenic construction may be far in the future, scenic planning goes hand in hand with track planning, **2**. It is important to leave enough space for structures, embankments, roads, streams, and bridges as you lay out track. You don't want to deal with vertical rock walls between tracks on different levels or have extensive inappropriate retaining walls. Think about the lay of the land as you approach final track design to avoid these often-jarring images that are rare in the real world.

## Earth moving

Study how a railroad cuts across a hillside as it climbs to a summit, **3**. Mother nature rarely provides smooth 1 percent grades right where a railroad needs them, so locating engineers search for a route that will allow a gradual climb along a hillside rather than straight up. A roadbed is cut into the hill at the desired grade, slowly climbing through cuts and fills, **4**, until the needed summit is reached.

One of the important dictums of earth moving is to balance cuts and fills. It is very expensive to haul dirt away from a construction site and dump it elsewhere, so excavated material is normally used close by. The roadbed will encounter humps and

**4**

A considerable amount of dirt was removed from the cut (distance at right) on the Western Maryland and used as fill in the foreground embankment. Note that, as an older fill, grass and foliage have taken root. *CJ Riley*

**Pinkerton Tunnel on the Baltimore & Ohio illustrates the depth of a cut before tunneling begins. The lack of hillside immediately above the portal is because the tunnel curves to the left into the face of the ridge. Note also the layering of the rock and the talus slopes of loose material at the bottom.** *CJ Riley*

**A Virginian & Ohio tunnel is bored through solid rock, so it does not need a portal. This HO scene illustrates a situation that, although not common, is used on the prototype when rock strata above is thick and strong.** *W. Allen McClelland*

gullies as it proceeds and the material cut from the humps will be deposited in the gullies. Likewise, material excavated from tunnels will have to be used somewhere. A good way to become familiar with the process would be to examine a recently constructed highway where the cuts and fills will be obvious, but a study of railroad photos will also add to your understanding.

Consciously make your scenery look as if a man-made grade was superimposed on its natural forms. Model cuts and fills and include an obvious line where the fill material meets the undulating natural grade. Have the roadbed builders excavate a cut into a hillside for some distance before the tunnel boring begins.

## Tunnels

A common realism killer on many layouts is a tunnel portal shoved directly against a steep dirt mountain face with little material directly above. Digging a cut is cheaper than tunneling, so crews would excavate as far as possible before beginning a tunnel, **5**. Yes, there are occasions where a track tunnels directly into a sheer rock cliff, but the critical terms are "sheer" and "rock," **6**.

Another unrealistic distraction for me is the proliferation of modeled rectangular tunnel portals with an opening cut in. I've seen a few such prototype portals in my life, but they normally would have retaining walls projecting out to the side, or to the

front, to hold back the sides of the excavation. More common in the area I model is a wide portal built into the sloping sides of the cut, thus holding back all the dirt above and beside the portal with the roadbed leading to it between increasingly higher slopes, **7**.

Also frequently missing in a model is the tunnel liner, a structural arch often of stone, brick, or concrete (sometimes timber in early days, but rare later because of the fire hazard) that continues the opening of the portal back into the tunnel. This liner supports the tunnel roof and protects the track from dirt and rock falls. A tunnel through solid rock may not need a liner and, in fact, might not even need a portal. An interesting detail is a

**7**

The opposite opening at Pinkerton has a cut-stone portal. The line was once double tracked but reduced to single track for better clearance. Note the tunnel name carved in the flat slab above the opening. The portal is fitted to the rock cut on either side, not just plastered against the mountain. The stone has been blackened by years of exposure to coal smoke and there's vegetation growing in the mortar joints. *CJ Riley*

bare tunnel opening under a substantial rock ledge, not uncommon in layered rock strata.

Don't forget other important features such as drainage ditches along the roadbed (tunnels can collect a lot of seepage) and details such as telltales, devices that warn trainmen on a car roof of impending low overhead clearance. These disappeared after safety regulations forced removal of roof-top running boards and the ladders that served them by the 1980s.

I recently saw a photo of a pair of modeled tunnel portals, slightly offset, where a stone retaining wall for a close-to-the-aisle portal was supporting the rock wall of the rearmost tunnel. Even if that could be engineered, why would it be done when a little more cut would eliminate that overhanging rock?

Another expense that railroads minimized are retaining walls, **8**. Occasional low and short walls may be used to protect stream beds, to hold back fill on a rocky cliff, separate slight grade changes in a tight yard or to solve other occasional problems. In an urban setting, where land is scarce and valuable, railroads often make extensive use of retaining walls rather than embankments, **9**, but if you model retaining walls higher than about 20

**8**

The 12-foot-tall retaining wall at left shows the large stones used by the Pennsylvania RR where the tracks are close to a street. A concrete cap flares outward so that the railing won't impede clearances. Note the signature Pennsy cast stanchions for the simple steel pipe railings. The small wall above illustrates how the stonework was built to follow the slope being retained. It is higher in the middle and slopes down naturally as the need fades away.

*Left: Larry Kline; Above: CJ Riley*

**9**

Here's an example of a poorly used retaining wall on an otherwise well-done railroad. It's not apparent what the wall is retaining since it abuts a massive rock formation. The bridge is just sitting on the "natural" rock with no abutment. There's a lack of continuity in the scene and no sense of the railroad being built through an existing natural environment. *CJ Riley*

**10**

The effects of uncontrolled water can be disastrous as here on the Western Maryland in West Virginia. The force of water runoff from a 1978 tropical storm scoured the ditches down to the base, nicely illustrating the depth of the ballast and roadbed. *CJ Riley*

**11**

I included water cascading from ditch runoff using a piece of monofilament fishing line running from a hole drilled in the tie end to another hole below. The line was coated with gloss gel medium with sparkling artificial snow crystals dusted on. The same resin as used in the creek forms the water in the ditch as well as that splashing and flowing down the rocky bank. *CJ Riley*

**12**

The WM needed to share a narrow valley with a small creek, so the water was controlled with a tie-box structure. The slope below was lined with stone (rip rap) to protect the soft fill from erosion. *CJ Riley*

feet, you will be stretching credibility. You might find an occasional massive retaining wall, but for maximum realism it's best to avoid such walls unless you can find specific examples on your prototype.

## Roadbed is scenery!

Drainage is extremely important in railroading. We'll touch on this subject under bridges later, but because a culvert is a short bridge, let's expand a bit. Drainage is a major concern, even on a backwoods logging line.

If rain water and snow melt aren't channeled away from the roadbed, serious damage and undermining of the track is guaranteed to happen. See the photo from the Western Maryland to understand the seriousness of this problem, **10**.

Yes, except for outdoor garden railroads or a plumbing leak, real drainage problems will not occur on our railroads. I did once hear about a bad plumbing leak that cascaded onto a model railroad and was channeled through the drainage systems to

the floor with minimal damage to structures and scenery. Obviously, the builder understood drainage. This won't happen to most of us, but proper drainage—culverts, ditches and stream beds—will greatly add to the sense of realism, **11**.

Drainage begins with trackside ditches, **12**. They are critical along the uphill side of the roadbed and both sides through cuts, but aren't necessary on fills, since the water naturally flows downhill away from the track, eventually soaking into the ground or

**13**

Culverts are placed wherever drainage is needed, such as on grades to move water running down a hill across the tracks. *CJ Riley*

**14**

Here's a natural scene with what is clearly man-made embankment. Note the color variations where material has been dumped down the slope, the variegated vegetation, and the wire fence separating the railroad's right-of-way from the consistent texture of the farmer's fallow field. *Paul Dolkos*

reaching a water course.

On a long grade, small culverts will be frequent, **13**, often every 100 feet, with more substantial culverts when crossing small water courses. A small trickle might call for a corrugated pipe, a rivulet a pipe with concrete headwalls, and a small creek might call for a stone arch or short timber trestle, leaving simple bridges for more substantial flows.

Don't assume, since your railroad runs through dry country, you don't need to worry about ditches and culverts. Even the Arizona desert is hit by occasional flash floods and an examination of prototype railroads in the region will reveal some surprisingly large culverts.

## The lay of the land

Land is not flat! Even land graded for a large parking lot is not truly flat, for drainage reasons, and Mother Nature abhors flat land as well as a vacuum. Realism can be greatly improved even on flat plywood layout if the land is subtly enhanced with little raised areas and dips. Good drainage necessitates that structures should be located on slightly raised areas, that railroads and roads will be raised above the

surrounding land, **14**, and streams will run below it. Using open benchwork makes the rolling countryside effect more easily achieved and thus it is advantageous, but all framing methods will allow some elevation change, **15**.

Steeper hillsides are common in much of the world and can be most advantageous in creating backdrops and screening imperfections. Natural soil will slope at about 45 degrees maximum, called the angle of repose. If there is rock, a slope can be steeper, up to vertical. In modeling, we can get away with steeper slopes, particularly when they are viewed straight on since the actual steepness is not apparent except from a side angle.

A real opportunity exists here to both save space and create an illusion. A very steep ridge up to eye level or more can be a simple slab of construction foam, and it could replace a painted backdrop (perhaps except for sky). If deciduous forests are being modeled, flat "puff ball" trees can be layered up the hill, getting smaller toward the top, and the illusion of distance is enhanced. Parts of smaller-scale structures set in the trees can augment the illusion. Foreground hillsides require more individual tree

modeling and more detail with ground cover. Lower, more rolling land can feature foreground trees in detail with the rest of the forest just tree tops.

Don't forget that a forest is not a manicured park and is much more than simply trees. There will be ground cover, dead leaves, fallen logs, stumps, dead trees, rocky outcroppings, low shrubbery or underbrush, animals, springs, creeks, and even (unfortunately) abandoned vehicles and junk. Going a step or two past a generic forest will boost the believability of the scene.

Open land is also not as straightforward as simple grassy fields. There are often several sizes of small stones mixed in with the dirt, patches of weeds, and occasional boulders. If you look at grass and weeds, you will see multiple colors and textures, not just an even green. That variation is easily duplicated and is critical to successful ground cover.

The best way to create believable ground cover is to start with a good base that is not dead flat and is painted a basic dirt color. Layers of dried real dirt that has been sifted into several sizes is lightly spread on a coating of white glue. A spray of wet water (water with a few added drops of dish detergent) sprayed on the dirt will help tie it down, along with some additional thinned white glue. Several layers of ground foam grasses and weeds along with bits of twine or other weed-making materials and some low shrubbery will give a realistic representation of ground cover, particularly in the foreground.

It is entirely appropriate to treat foreground, middle ground and background differently. Closeup scenes require more detail and accuracy, while farther back the scene can be simplified. Think again about scale distance. A foot back from the viewer is 48 feet in O scale, 87 feet in HO, 160 feet in N, etc. How much texture do you perceive 48 or 87 feet away? Colors begin to fade because of haze in the air, trees become less complex, and the detail on vehicles and structures are much less obvious.

Take advantage of this visual phenomena in your modeling. Put lots of effort into foreground trees and grasses and place your best figures and vehicles up front. Structures are easily seen in the foreground and they should be more fully detailed, perhaps with peeling paint and interior details. Simplifying your scenery toward the rear saves time, money and hassle while increasing realism.

## Rockwork

The temptation to create massive rock faces dwells inside many of us, but we must all be careful lest the evil force of the rock ogre take over. Yes, the Rocky Mountains are well named, and modelers of that area can be excused for the worship of rock castings piled one upon the other. The rest of us must be more prudent.

I am not a geologist and not an expert on the art of mineralogy, but I am aware of how rock types vary between regions. The layered limestone under eastern Kentucky, **16**, has a different appearance from the folded sandstone of the Appalachians and the hard volcanic rock of the Canadian shield or the Cascades. Learn at least a little about the rock that you will represent before you make even one casting.

What is the predominant rock type in your area? Volcanic igneous rocks such as granite? Layered sediments such as sandstone or coal? Metamorphic rock such as marble? Are the layers horizontal, uplifted or folded? What are the predominant colors and other obvious colors?

This is a very simplified view of geology, but perhaps it's a good start on creating believable rockwork. It's easy to spend some time online or with a book in order to better understand

and make the appropriate selections in texture, color and formation of the rock you want to model.

Among the most glaring incongruities I have seen are giant slabs of almost rectangular stone forming a cliff, or little bumps of stone randomly plastered on a hillside. Such casual uses of stone castings or carvings are a distraction at best, because they are not obviously natural. Likewise, beware of entire mountainsides that are nothing but rock castings, with no respite: no ledges with bits of grass or foliage, no trees clinging to a crevice, no color changes, no layering of any kind. These anomalies may occur occasionally in nature, but you would risk revocation of your modeler's license if you were guilty of not modeling from the prototype.

I'm trying not to be overly critical here, but to encourage you to pay attention and think about rocks. I had such an epiphany many years ago when visiting a local model railroad. The modeler had done a nice job of having a layer of stone protruding from the side of a railroad cut, with the soil, root structure and natural growth above it, a realistic talus slope below, and with obvious erosion patterns. I was blown away by the rightness of this scene (in West Virginia) and never modeled rock casually again. After that visit, I noticed

**15**

Changing elevations helps provide realism. Here Paul Dolkos has carefully modeled a town scene with a wooded slope to the tracks, obvious drainage patterns to the concrete culvert at the lower left, and the road curving into town from the bridge. The coloration of the structures and the white steepled church in the background add to the believability of this New England town. *Paul Dolkos*

**16**

This cut illustrates the layering of sedimentary rock, where a thick sedimentary layer is at track level and a soil slope with intermittent layers of rock rise at a shallow angle above. This is an old cut, evidenced by the considerable foliage taking root in the slope and a fair amount of debris laying in the ditch. *CJ Riley*

Streams flow at different rates depending on season and rainfall. This stream bed is much wider than the present flow of the current. Large areas of rock and gravel, interspersed with trees and shrubs, occupy the inside of the curve of Red Creek in West Virginia. *CJ Riley*

that pattern regularly along highways and railroads and then as typical rock outcroppings high on the ridges above rivers in the Mountain State.

Don't take this to mean that railroads never cut through solid rock, but the blasting and moving of that rock is expensive and would be avoided if possible. On the other hand, when building a roadbed through Colorado's Animas Canyon the rock blasting is inevitable. Just study your prototype railroad or region and model accordingly.

## Modeling water

There are as many ways to model water as there are water forms. Water can be anything from a puddle, to a pond, to a trickle, a creek, a stream, **17**, or a river, **18**. It can be still, be tumbling over rocks, cascading over a ledge or simply flowing as a river. The appearance of each of these differs by region and topography, so proper depiction entails different methodologies.

A creek in West Virginia is normally wide and shallow with a gravel bottom and an occasional rock ledge. A creek in the Midwest, **19**, may flow more slowly and deeply,

As streams flow downhill, they grow in volume as they join each other, often splashing over and through rocks and cascading over ledges as with this stream. *CJ Riley*

**19**

This resin-based stream represents deep, silty water. The ripples are gloss gel medium, stippled a brush atop the resin. Although the stream runs directly into the backdrop, the joint is somewhat disguised by the foliage, implying a turn in the stream. It's not a perfect illusion, but easier than disguising a hard edge with the backdrop. *CJ Riley*

**20**

Paul Scoles used resin to represent slow-moving water in this gravel-bottomed small stream. Note the larger boulders projecting above the water and the indication of water flow implied by white paint. The bank has broken stone on one side with sand and smaller stones on the other. *Paul Scoles*

**21**

Apparent water color varies considerably, from blue to silty tan to greenish to gray, depending on the sky color, bottom (bed) color, dissolved materials in the water, algae, or reflections from the trees along the shore. *CJ Riley*

meandering through an almost flat countryside and have a muddy or sandy bottom, with overhanging banks. I know these are generalities, but you must understand what is typical for the region you intend to represent before you can model it rather than a generic

stream, **20**.

Colors vary widely. We often think of water as being blue, **21**, which—because of sky reflection—it often appears. Water itself, of course, is usually clear. But it can take on the color of reflected sky (which can vary

greatly between sunny and cloudy days) or neighboring objects (trees, rock faces, etc.), the color of mud or sediment in the water, or the color of the streambed or lake bed or bottom. See Chapter 8 for more discussion of colors.

**Larger bodies of water are easily modeled with multiple coats of varnish or gloss medium over an appropriately painted dead-level surface such as plywood (with the grain well sealed). This harbor scene, with bulkheads and piers, forgoes the need for stream banks and a transition in apparent depth.** *Fred Gill*

It is often recommended that you prepare a plaster or plywood bed for your stream, paint it black in the middle shading toward tan at the banks, and pour a resin stream. This might work well for a Midwestern or generic creek, and certainly might be good for a larger river, but it would not be a common creek in the Alleghenies where the gravel is often visible on the edges of a wide stream bed with the water flow toward the center. At bends, the water is on the outside of the curve with lots of gravel on the inside. Occasionally, the stream encounters a solid rock ledge, cascades over it into a deep pool and then proceeds normally.

This may not be the kind of stream you are used to, and that is my point. Investigate the streams in the area you will model and proceed accordingly. Don't assume that clear resin is the only material: sealed and painted plywood with gloss medium can represent rough, deep water;

clear plastic sheet painted on the bottom and installed over a modeled underwater perimeter can capture a nice pond or deep stream; and even resin can be coated with gloss gel to create waves and ripples.

Don't forget that streams may have logs, cattails, reeds, lily pads, beaver, frogs, waterfowl, rhododendron and trees overhanging the water—even fish if you are so inclined. Fast water can be formed with clear silicone caulk, Christmas "snow" glitter, or a material I have discovered called Golden Gel Medium: Glass Bead Gel, which is a form of artists' medium that goes on white but dries frothy and glittery.

Like all other aspects of the hobby, do some research into materials (visit an artist's supply or craft store), study photos, and just look at water. Understanding what it is doing will help you build more realistic water scenes, **22**.

## Trees

Another area of our hobby that has shown great advancement is the modeling of trees, **23**. Once we had only weeds: spirea, goldenrod, Queen Anne's lace, and other vaguely tree-like natural growth. Then came Norwegian lichen, usually in vivid colors, from the hobby shop and we old timers thought we had it made.

The search for more realism then led us to cast-metal, then plastic tree trunk armatures that were covered with a fine netting and ground foam for leaves. Now we have many materials and techniques for modeling trees, letting us model specific species if we desire. Granted, if one is modeling an eastern deciduous forest, then individual trees of specific species may not be reasonable since, except in the foreground, all we see is the tree canopy—where puff-ball trees come in handy.

As in all the other areas of a model

**23**

A well-modeled forest floor is most obvious in this late autumn scene. Pulverized tree leaves are an effective and economical ground cover under trees, but don't forget to include fallen branches and twigs. While this scene conveys November, this texture is appropriate under trees in any season. *Paul Dolkos*

**24**

Steep ridges can be modeled with sloped sheet foam and flat "puffball" trees, layered like reversed shingles and getting smaller as the apparent distance increases. The foliage is oversprayed with rail brown to tone down the colors, and much green still exists. Foreground trees are three-dimensional and the most distant ridge is cardboard with coarse ground foam attached and oversprayed with dark gray to force the perspective. The paper backdrop is curving around a post at this point. *CJ Riley*

railroad, avoiding the generic in favor of the specific will greatly benefit the realism and sense of rightness of the scene. Modeling a specific tree species can be as simple as including the correct bark texture and color, along with the overall shape of the tree structure. More such data can be found at a library that has a copy of *Architectural Graphic Standards*.

Studying trees has the same benefit as studying rock formations or weathering patterns. One doesn't need to be an arborist to make an excellent tree model, but an understanding of basic shapes, textures and coloration will make the job easier. Do the branches of that evergreen sweep upward like a white pine or downward like a western red cedar? Is the foliage of a deciduous tree vase-shaped like an American elm or round, like a maple, ash, or linden? Rectangular like a white pine (vertical) or white oak (horizontal) or conical like a hemlock or fir? Is the bark textured or smooth, gray or red?

Such understandings will make your important specimen trees recognizable and believable. Not all the trees need to be this carefully modeled, but foreground trees, particularly if standing alone or near an important

structure or other scenic highlight, add a great deal to the realism factor. Middle-ground trees may be less detailed and background trees even less so. Distant hillsides or ridges can make use of puffballs, torn furnace filters or other shortcuts that imply much more detail than actually exists, **24**.

It is an accepted truth of our hobby that the many facets of layout building must eventually come together to make a whole. A layout builder should work toward a level of finish on each component that supports the vision of the completed work. If the goal is a believable operating transportation system, then understanding and replicating the prototype in every facet must be the focus of the work. That focus applies equally to locomotives, rolling stock, structures, weathering, and operations.

But perfection in these areas quickly fades if the scenery lacks an equal attention to the prototype. Generic scenery is better than none, but good replication of ground cover textures and appropriate rockwork, topped off with trees and foliage that represent specific species will certainly raise the level of the sense of "rightness."

## LEARNING POINTS →

**1.** Scenery around railroad roadbed should reflect how the earth was moved to construct the grade.

**2.** Cuts and fills should be modeled in a way that illustrates the original and new land forms for maximum realism.

**3.** Ditches for drainage should be included where appropriate, along with culverts.

**4.** Land is never truly flat.

**5.** Tunnel portals should be placed in cuts.

6. Rock can be layered or monolithic, depending on the type.

**7.** Ridges viewed head-on can be much steeper than in the real world.

**8.** Water comes in many colors and textures.

**9.** Many varieties of foliage, plants, and trees grow next to natural water, seeking the moisture.

1

CHAPTER FOUR

# Mirrors for illusion

John Allen was a pioneer in the use of mirrors. This shot of his Great Divide yard is a classic example of a large mirror to double the apparent size of a yard. Look at the large red brick building in the back at left and the joint becomes more obvious. The sides of the mirror are screened by the tall buildings and the top is camouflaged by the backdrop smoke painted over the mirror's top edge.

*John Allen; Peter Prunka collection*

The first use of mirrors on a model railroad is lost to time, but the legendary John Allen used several and his oft-published photos well illustrated their advantages, **1**. They are great for expanding scenes—creating the illusion of a larger space than is actually there.

A key in realism when using mirrors is that people should never be reflected. This test shot, however, shows that the effects will be good with the buildings toward the bottom of the mirror, with the structures enhanced by their apparent doubling the size. *CJ Riley*

The front edge of the mirror was moved forward ½" and trimmed with wood. That angle is noticeable when the track near the caboose on the bridge is compared with the reflection, though the modeled tracks continue past the mirror through a notch. The yard tracks meet the mirror at 90 degrees. A large bead of caulking was applied to the joint with the backdrop and painted over to help hide the rear reflection gap. *CJ Riley*

Large mirrors can be placed at the end of a yard so that the length of the tracks and the rolling stock is doubled. Smaller mirrors are also very useful. There are only two rules for successful use of a mirror: It must be positioned to not reflect a viewer, and it must be placed precisely 90 degrees to abutting tracks, streams, roads, and (in most cases) structures, **2**.

Seeing one's own giant face floating over your scenery is disorienting as well as illusion-busting. Having tracks make a sharp angular bend at the mirror creates an impossible visual anomaly. However, careful and creative mirror placement can project light into dark corners, continue sidings "through" a wall, enlarge the apparent size of a structure interior, or create numerous other illusions, **3**.

The end-of-a-yard trick is well known and obvious, but there are some considerations. While nothing can be done about the reversed rolling stock lettering in the reflection, structure signs are another matter. If a sign is close to the mirror, the reflected image will be very prominent and noticeable.

I once planned, but never carried out, a scene where a car was visible only in the end-of-yard mirror, obscured from normal view. It would

have been lettered in reverse and occasionally assigned for pick up by an unsuspecting operator who would waste much time trying to find a way to reach the car. Unfair, perhaps, but amusing to the operators in the know.

There are two types of mirrors: front-reflecting and rear-reflecting. The common mirror familiar to everyone has the reflecting surface at the back of the glass, leaving a gap equal to the thickness of the glass (commonly ⅛" or so). Front-reflecting mirrors eliminate this gap but can be much

more expensive, and the fragile surface is subject to damage from cleaning and accidents.

Until recently, I had seen only rear reflecting mirrors used on model railroads and, since the only real disadvantage is the perceived "gap", we will explore solutions to that problem. See the photos and captions for details.

## Bridge
I wanted a highway bridge to run along a mirror, crossing the tracks, as a sleight-of-hand diversion, **4**.

The almost-finished scene shows the effectiveness of the mirror. *CJ Riley*

**5**

The addition of a large industrial structure helped to minimize the symmetry problem. The permanent "half bridge" is in place and the black paint/ivy on the pier to hide the glass thickness are obvious. The head on vehicle collision helps to distract the viewer's eye as will a yet to be built industry in the open space. The safety sign on the bridge and the radiator steam help to disguise the gaps in the bridge structure. *CJ Riley*

**6**

With the bridge removed, the illusions are clearer. The pier between the buildings show that the final gray was more successful in minimizing the gap. The space for lease sign is visible correctly in the mirror because it was lettered in reverse on the model. The open area will be filled with an industry and further screen the gaps. *CJ Riley*

This meant the bridge, piers and any vehicles would be reflected, as well as the tracks. Since these items would be doubled by the reflection, **5**, I split the bridge down the center line and cut the piers and vehicles. While this scene was intended to distract the eye from the mirror, many visible gaps were created that threatened to spoil the illusion, so I created additional diversions and illusions.

First up were the stone piers which were split plaster castings. A basic principle of stagecraft is to make everything that was to be hidden from the audience black, so I painted the cut face black. When I set the piers against the mirror. I had a ⅛" black line running down the stonework. There is an old saying that doctors can bury their mistakes, architects can only plant ivy. Extrapolating that saying to model railroading, any visual problem can be fixed with a little ivy. White glue and ground foam were added to the stone face, leaving the little black line through the ivy. So, to hide that line, I applied a little ivy to the mirror itself. Now I had ivy hanging in the air, with another bit of it ⅛" away (other side of the glass) separated by that pesky black line.

Starting over, the abutting edge of the pier was painted a lighter shade of the stone color, the lack of light in the glass meant the black line had

**7**

The gray on the connecting bridge edge is a little light, but it's still an improvement and the caulking bead is more subdued. Note the lettering style chosen had a slant to the left on the "O", an error I wouldn't repeat. I should have used a mirror under the bridge to lighten the black hole effect, but that problem is much less obvious from a normal viewing angle. The business name was chosen so that it would reflect properly. *CJ Riley*

disappeared and the gap, although still noticeable, had diminished considerably. I would depend on freight cars and structures, along with details on the bridge to help divert the eye, **6**.

For the bridge, there was that old gap running down the center of the deck. An easy fix, indeed, was a piece of white map tape along the vertical edge. The color was reflected in the mirror creating a center line that visually filled the gap. The bridge portal had a black/yellow "half chevron" (paper on thin styrene) added across the face and a safety slogan sign glued directly on the mirror face above the bridge, screening the gaps in the truss cross members.

There were still the problems of vehicles and people being duplicated and everything being on only one side of the road. What to do? A traffic accident! A farmer's pickup truck on the way to market with crates of geese wandered across the center line and collided head-on with a car. Crates fell off the truck, geese escaped and were

**8**

The normal view of Paul Scoles' town of Silverado shows how the mirror (behind the bridge and passenger car) is a minor element in the scene, screened here by the foreground action and the bridge. *Paul Scoles*

**9**

In a more typical view, the mirror in not obvious but it avoids the black hole syndrome in the tunnel, completes the junction, and implies that the track continues down the valley. *Paul Scoles*

everywhere, while a damaged radiator sent clouds of steam into the air.

This solution used all the tricks. The vehicles were split and there isn't much to be done about the joint other than diversion of the eye. A goose (two geese) on the truck roof and several men standing around the carnage are a good diversion and the steam, painted on the mirror obscures the gap in the portal chevrons. The figures were painted differently on the front and back, so different people appear to be standing on both sides of the wreck. A goose up on the bridge truss is another diversion.

A nearby multi-story warehouse building was located near the mirror and thus would be reflected. The first need was a name for the building that would reflect properly (a palindrome). I made a list of symmetrical letters: A, H, I, M, O, T, U, V, W, X, Y. I was aware of the classic palindrome "OTTO" and quickly determined a name ending in "OV" would be very Russian so Otto Vomittimov became the owner of a liquor warehouse. I needed a bridge to span the roadway and connect the upper floor with the reflection, but when I lettered the first half of Otto's last name on the bridge it was Vomit and the liquor business was quickly changed to be a general warehouse, **7**.

I was careful to paint the abutting surface in a lighter gray, but I didn't take enough care with selection of a type face and realized, too late, the lettering had a slight slant to the right

which reflected as a slant to the left. It is a subtlety, but I am always aware of it. That is something to consider when selecting a typeface

I added a sign on the real structure facing the mirror and lettered it in reverse by using decals applied "face down". Therefore, the illusion of a large structure (no mirror) is reinforced when one reads the lease ad in the reflection and the backward sign cannot be seen.

Yes, everything else in that scene is also reflected, but the distance from the mirror is doubled in the reflection and the bridge scene, along with freight cars in the yard and other structures, attract the eye away from those other images—much the way a backdrop fades away when the trains are the focus, **8, 9**.

Where a bridge is near a wall, the scene below can be visually extended by placing a mirror behind the bridge with the mirror top screened by the bridge structure. Likewise, a track ending at a wall can be set into a short tunnel against a small mirror. Properly done, the road, stream, or tracks spanned by the bridge will appear to continue up a valley.

A broken mirror is rumored to bring bad luck, but the shards can be a boon to the modeler. While large mirrors can be very effective in doubling the size of yards and industries, smaller mirrors can also be very useful. In addition to reflecting images, mirrors also reflect light and, carefully placed, will prevent dark areas where there are openings,

such as where roads disappear into trees or the area under bridges near a backdrop, **10**.

I have successfully used small mirrors to give the effect of a stream continuing "through" a painted

**10**

A mirror can help solve a prickly scenery challenge. Here, a stream runs into the backdrop at the end of a peninsula. A scrap of mirror under the covered bridge reflects the hidden stream bank and carries the stream out of sight. Without the mirror, there would be a black hole under the bridge and little sense of distance. *CJ Riley*

The paintbrush points to the bottom of a mirror shard buried in the trees that continues the mining road back around the ridge line. *CJ Riley*

## FRONT-REFLECTING MIRRORS

Front-reflecting mirrors are available, but can be expensive (especially in large sizes). Other options include a sheet of highly polished stainless steel (expensive) or reflective Mylar film (difficult to mount to a rigid surface without bumps), but the best method I've seen appears to be the use of thicker, more rigid Mylar type product.

A related material called Silver Metalized Dura-Lar is available in 50 mil (.050") thickness. Although it's not quite self-supporting, it's easily mounted to any rigid material such as plywood, hardboard, or drywall with double-faced tape at the top, allowing it to hang free and flat. Just be careful to keep spatters and dirt off the surface, as repetitive cleaning will likely cause problems.

You may find other similar products available locally or online from commercial plastic suppliers or sign-making houses. Don't be afraid to experiment with alternatives—the world of plastics is constantly changing.

The line splitting the Walthers warehouse is all but invisible with the Dura-Lar mirror. You can see the butt joint with the wall above and a line across the platform to the left of the boxcar. All the other cautions regarding reflections of the viewer, right-angle abutments to the mirror, and signs still apply. *Steve Hinksman*

backdrop. The curving stream meets a mirror which has the edges screened by adjacent trees, so the stream appears to curve away from the viewer and disappear around a bend. I have also had a dirt road, **11**, that previously ended in a pitch-black hole come alive when a small mirror was placed in the trees. More than just continuing the road, the bright image in the mirror gave the effect of a clearing beyond the trees rather than a basement wall. These are subtle effects, but are incredibly effective and eliminate many distractions, **12**.

A mirror is also useful for implying trackage leading to a structure that exists only on the backdrop. This is a technique useful for any industry that is so large as to overwhelm the model railroad. Steel mills, chemical plants, refineries, and the like can be included on the backdrop or just implied with a gated fence and sign. A short track leading to a mirror (which extends the siding out of sight) provides switching opportunities without a space-eating model.

There are screening devices other than trees that can hide the edges of mirrors. Buildings can hide the sides; bridges, hanging signs, or other overhead structures can hide the top. A tall chimney or the slope of a hillside cut or any vertical object will work, but remember there must be two of them unless the item is split in half. A tunnel portal set a short distance from the wall with a mirror at the wall will give the appearance of a track continuing off into the distance, or a large culvert will give the appearance of water continuing, **13**, as will track ending at a mirror that is screened with a cut or trees. This can be very useful where a track represents a branch line and the track is used for staging an inbound train at the beginning of a session or parking an outbound train at the end of an operating session.

Properly and creatively used, mirrors can be very useful in creating many illusions that, subtle or obvious, will add richness and texture to a model railroad and thus add to the sense of rightness.

The St. Nicholas Breaker is modeled as a cutout on the backdrop and the siding leading to it ends at a mirror. The pair of Reading Baldwin switchers seems to be pulling a cut of loads from the facility, but is, in fact, a single loco and its reflection in the mirror. With the Baldwins removed (right), the full reflection is seen, including some distracting yard trackage. This is not visible at normal viewing angles, but provides a cautionary tale. *Two photos: Mike Rinkunas*

This underpass was modeled after one on the Pennsylvania RR in Edgewood, Pennsylvania. The masonry is composed of individual styrene stones on a sheet styrene base. The mirror is halfway back and angled to represent the curved road on the prototype and to minimize the chance of seeing a face reflected.
*CJ Riley*

## LEARNING POINTS →

**1.** Mirrors must be placed so that viewers don't see their own reflections.

**2.** Objects abutting a mirror must meet the mirror at 90 degrees to avoid a "kink," unless a special effect is desired.

**3.** Rear-reflecting mirrors are less expensive and more durable than front-reflecting mirrors, but the thickness of the glass affects the reflection.

**4.** An inexpensive front-reflecting mirror can be created using 50-mil Dura-Lar, a Mylar type material affixed to a smooth solid backing such as styrene or hardboard.

**5.** Small mirrors will reflect light into the interior of a dark area, increasing apparent depth and realism.

**6.** Screening or hiding the edges of mirrors is important.

1

# CHAPTER FIVE

# Installing accurate bridges

A modeled deck plate girder bridge carries a slightly curving track. The girder sits on a rocking shoe on a stone abutment. The tie cribbing retaining the roadbed would not be as common as additional stone. The timbers along the tracks carry a heavy water flow to a scupper that still needs to have the cascade modeled. *CJ Riley*

What model railroader doesn't dream of trains moving across massive bridges or towering trestles? Bridges are highlights of both model and prototype railroads and are often favorite locales for photographers of both, **1**. However, the proper installation and use of bridges unfortunately eludes many modelers. Knowing how prototype bridges are used and what type of bridge is appropriate for a given installation goes a long way toward realistic scenes.

Although I'm not an engineer by training, my profession as an architect gives me an understanding of basic structural principles, and I've made a point of studying bridge structure. I'm often appalled when viewing model railroads (via photos or in person) where all too often I'm confronted with an improbable or even structurally impossible bridge of which the builder may be quite proud.

The challenge for modelers is that bridges, unlike freight cars and locomotives, are not standardized pieces of equipment ordered from a builder's catalog. Each bridge is normally designed and fabricated to suit its situation, although railroads often recycled older removed bridges by moving them to other suitable locations. There are enough model bridges of common designs commercially available (particularly in HO scale) that extensive kitbashing or scratchbuilding is rarely necessary. Still, a basic understanding of bridge design will add greatly to one's ability to effectively model them, as well as to modify a bridge to suit a different situation, span or even scale, **2**.

Bridges sit in plain view, unmoving, and are visual highlights, so they are frequently subject to the close-up scrutiny of visitors. If the bridge structure is obviously too light, there are not proper abutments (an all too common occurrence), or the bridge is a poor choice for the location, realism and the "sense of rightness" quickly fade. A single chapter of a book can't do proper justice to a comprehensive study of bridges, but I'll endeavor to provide enough knowledge to avoid glaring errors. I suggest perusal of *The Bridge & Trestle Handbook for Model Railroads* by Paul Mallery (originally published by Carstens in 1972; its fourth edition is available from White River Productions). You can also check out *The Model Railroader's Guide to Bridges, Trestles & Tunnels*, by Jeff Wilson (Kalmbach).

There are many styles and uses for railroad bridges, **3**. The most obvious use is for the railroad to pass over a highway, waterway, valley, or another railroad. The first principle of bridge

**2** John Allen was renowned for his spectacular bridges, but a modeler seriously interested in a sense of rightness would do well to avoid the spectacular in favor of the more likely. While John knew enough engineering to make his bridges feasible, he commonly stretched their probability with his choices of bridge type and/or location. The Scalp Mountain arch is an excellent example, spectacular but all but impossible to erect. The concrete pier under the deck bridge at left stretches height limits, and the girders spring from a difficult-to-support stone arch. Nonetheless, I admire John's modeling and I make these criticisms more as an example of something best avoided if a sense of rightness is important to you and not as a dislike of his work. *John Allen; Peter Prunka collection*

**3** Longer expanses may need a sequence of spans and they need not match in size or type. This is the Louisville & Nashville's crossing of the Ohio River at Henderson, Ky., on a series of five through truss spans totalling 2,655 feet. *Louisville & Nashville*

4

When a bridge interrupts a navigable waterway, accommodation must be made for marine traffic. Bridges can lift up, tip back or pivot to clear the channel. This double deck swing bridge, by necessity a cantilever type, pivots over the center pier to clear the channel. A highway runs on the upper level and the railroad on the lower. Note the pilings that protect the pier from errant boats or debris and the spindly access walkway. *CJ Riley collection*

5

A deck bridge is almost always the prototype's first choice and should be the modeler's as well. Since this stream is not navigable by commercial vessels, clearance is not an issue, so the Western Maryland chose twin steel plate girder deck spans for economy and ease of erection at this stream crossing. *CJ Riley*

6

This twin-span steel truss bridge shudders under the pounding of a Reading 4-8-4 dressed as Chesapeake & Ohio no. 614 as it storms across the Allegheny River in Pittsburgh with a Chessie Steam Special in tow. Note the riveted lattice-work columns and the steel plates reinforcing the corners of the cross members and column bases, as well as the smaller guard rails between the tracks. While it is unlikely a model railroad builder would need such a massive bridge, it is worth understanding the how and why of its construction. *CJ Riley*

design is to minimize the span length (opening), even if it takes several short bridges to cross a gap. The height, while often determined by adjacent geography, would normally be only as high as clearance requires so that material use is minimized. A bridge over a navigable waterway must be high enough to allow passing craft to clear (Coast Guard regulations), or else be moveable by either pivoting or lifting to provide the necessary clear opening, **4**.

## Bridge types

Let's begin with choosing a proper bridge. There are important reasons why an engineer chooses a bridge type: to balance cost, maintain necessary clearances, accessibility for construction, materials or labor available, and desired life span. Bridges can be of deck construction, where the track runs above the structure, **5**, or through, where the track runs between the major structural members, **6**. A stone arch bridge is an early example of a deck bridge, as is a wooden trestle, **7**. But steel quickly replaced these materials and is now normally used in the form of either truss bridges or plate girders for the deck support, although there are a few examples of steel arch railroad bridges, **8**.

The earliest railroads used wood for simple bridges, **9**, and stone where longer spans were needed. A creek

**7**

Low wood pile trestles are still common, and are a simple type of deck bridge. A Chicago, Burlington & Quincy steam excursion crosses a stream and gulley in northern Illinois in 1958. *John Pickett*

might be spanned by a single stone arch, but as many arches as necessary can be strung together to cross a broad valley. Stone arches can be set on tall piers if needed to reach the roadbed height, but the temporary wooden falsework needed to support the stonework until the keystone is set and the arch is stabilized adds a major cost. Stone arches are very stable and long-lived, but labor intensive and thus expensive to build. Their use did not prevail after steel became common. Several Eastern railroads made extensive use of stone arch bridges in railroading's early days and many of those bridges are still in use, carrying the weight and speed of modern equipment more than 150 years after their construction, **10**.

As railroads pushed westward,

**8**

The Santa Fe built a cantilevered arch bridge across Canyon Diablo, near Two Guns Arizona. Since the canyon depth proscribed false work for temporary support during construction, the steel framing of each half arch can "balance" on the concrete piers. The short middle span is then eased into place to complete the arching action. *Ivan Safyan Abrams*

**9**

The Everett & Monte Cristo crossed this wood truss deck bridge in the 1800s. Wood railroad bridges became rare by the early 1900s. *Di Voss collection*

**10**

Amtrak's St. Louis to New York City "National Limited" crosses the Pennsylvania RR Spruce Creek stone arch viaduct near Huntington, Pa. *Ivan Safyan Abrams*

**A fine example of a late wooden trestle is on the West Side Lumber Co. in California. Note that while the trestle is curved, there is a straight section in the middle to accommodate the creek crossing.** *John West*

wooden trestles became common since timber was plentiful and erection speed was more important than permanence. There are many spectacular examples of tall timber trestles in the early days as well as on later logging lines, **11**, but tall trestles shouldn't be the first choice for a mainline modeler of the 1940s and later. I understand the appeal of these intricate structures and know the temptation is there, but modern diesels on mainline tall wooden trestles are an anomaly usually best avoided. Unless modeling a prototype that used them, it's best to stick with low trestles over creeks or as approaches to steel bridges. Those uses are still somewhat common and won't attract the "bridge police."

As bridge spans increased, through and deck bridges of timber truss construction with iron rod tension members became common, but timber is susceptible to rot and deterioration so wood was quickly replaced by iron and then steel. Steel plate girders are more common as deck bridges, **12**, but if used as a through bridge, extensive cross framing under the deck is needed

**This straightforward single-span plate girder has a fill at the right end which comes from a cut just out of sight. There is a rocking bearing fixture, and the rail is spiked to proper bridge ties.** *CJ Riley*

13

14

This new multi-span through plate-girder bridge shows the tight spacing of bridge ties compared to standard track, as well as the extensive diagonal bracing. *Missouri-Kansas-Texas*

The Western Maryland's Salisbury Viaduct carries the railroad across the broad valley of the Casselman River. It now carries the Great Allegheny Passage Trail. *Western Maryland Historical Society photo; CJ Riley collection*

to support the roadbed (these bridges can have ballasted decks or the ties can be secured to longitudinal stringers). Angled braces reinforce the girders along the inside of each side, **13**. Through bridges are wider than deck bridges to provide equipment clearance. The same rules apply to steel truss bridges of both varieties.

A very wide and/or deep valley is typically crossed by a steel trestle

(viaduct) consisting of spaced lightly framed steel towers or stone or concrete piers supporting a series of deck plate girders, **14**. The towers can be of considerable height and there is no limit to the width of the crossing. If waterways or roads need to be spanned, a deeper plate girder or appropriate truss of a longer span can be spliced in to do the job.

Concrete is a material best reserved

for piers and abutments, although there have been a few concrete arch bridges, primarily built in the early 20th century, **15**. Shorter concrete railroad spans aren't common, but they can sometimes be found crossing over highways, **16**, or narrow waterways. Decorative concrete spans over highways sometimes aren't what they seem—often the concrete sides are merely decorative panels covering up

15

16

Concrete arch bridges are relatively rare, but impressive. Here the Kansas City Southern's Southern Belle crosses the railroad's viaduct near Kansas City. The deck is ballasted. *Kansas City Southern*

Concrete bridges became popular for highway crossings in the early 20th century. Many were not truly concrete, but instead steel bridges with concrete side panels. This is on Atlantic Coast Line in Florence, S.C. *Atlantic Coast Line*

**A longer span would require a truss bridge and here, at Davidson Canyon, near Tucson Ariz., the Southern Pacific built a multiple-span steel deck truss.** *Ivan Safyan Abrams*

conventional plate-girders or steel I-beams. If you're planning to model a concrete railroad bridge, it's wise to check prototype photos for accuracy.

## Simple rules for believable bridges

A deck bridge should be first choice for any railroad bridge, **17**. Deck bridges are easier and cheaper to build than through bridges, and they avoid clearance problems. Limitations in span length can be ameliorated by building multiple spans on piers or supports (which can be steel, concrete, stone, or—rarely in modern times—wood). There must be adequate clearance, if required, for boats or vehicles to pass below, **18**, or above a waterway that runs high in flood season and would be a risk to a deck bridge. In

general, remember that the longer the individual span, the more significant structure is required for the bridge.

Through bridges are used only when clearance needs or longer spans required them. The extra expense precludes casual use of a through bridge, either plate girder or truss, unless there are other important factors. Unfortunately for modelers, the easy availability of cheap plastic through plate-girder bridges with flat, thin decks and no bracing has produced a plague of unrealistic models, namely excessive clearance below, having no visible cross bracing under the deck (made all-the-more obvious by the visibility of the underside), and often no visible pedestals, leaving the impression that the bridge is simply hanging from the track (or that the

ends are just resting on the neighboring scenery).

Arch bridges are far down the list, except for stone arch bridges built in the early days of railroad construction. Masonry arches are more frequently found as single-arch culverts (sometimes over roads, **19**) or tunnel portals and linings. True steel-arch construction is very expensive and thus limited to long spans over steep chasms with solid rock sides to support the outward thrust of the arch.

In most cases, for extremely long spans where multiple piers and segments are impractical, a cantilever design would likely be chosen, **20**. The principle of a cantilever is that it only requires support on one end (a conventional truss bridge requires support at each end). A pier near

**18**

A four-span plate girder deck bridge on concrete piers carries the Nicholas, Fayette & Greenbrier across the Cherry River in West Virginia. Note the rounded concrete piers that help the water to flow around. Some piers have pointed ("cutwater") edges facing upstream for the same purpose. *CJ Riley*

**19**

Don't forget that not all rural roads cross the tracks at grade. Minor underpasses can be a very nice addition to a model railroad. Note the clearance and narrow opening warnings, the pipe railing, the efflorescence stains and the foliage along the base and overhanging the stone wing walls. *CJ Riley*

**20**

each shoreline supports a cantilever projecting toward the middle (and usually a shorter one toward the shore). Usually a conventional truss bridge is placed at the middle of the span, connecting the cantilever on each end.

Keep in mind that a modeled bridge can be inappropriate even if built to prototype standards if it is used where the prototype would not place it. For example, a multi-span through truss bridge on a spur to a local coal dealer would be a glaring model anomaly. When in doubt it's usually best to model the typical rather than the unusual.

Also remember that railroads *do not* use suspension bridges. The dynamic loads of a moving train make this type of bridge highly impractical.

Another no-no is using curved

When Pittsburgh & Lake Erie in 1907 built a new bridge across the Ohio River at Beaver, Pa., the U.S. Army Corps of Engineers demanded an unobstructed 700-foot channel with 90-foot clearance and would not allow temporary falsework in the channel during construction. This made a cantilever bridge necessary. Great anchor arms sit on stone piers at each side of the 700 foot channel, their massive weight necessary to balance the span trusses as they were extended from each side until finally meeting at a conventional truss section in the middle of the span. The south cantilever of the bridge (above) nicely illustrates how the anchor arms allow the steel to be erected over the channel without support. The Beaver River is seen flowing into the Ohio in the background. *Both: Pittsburgh & Lake Erie*

**21**

Here's how to curve a bridge: The two girder spans are each straight as the track curves above, although skewed to match the stream bed. Each girder has appropriate shoes, sliding on the center pier and rocking on the ends. The abutments are stone but the center pier is concrete, implying a modernization of the structure. This pier is a wood block covered with drywall compound scored with "form board lines" to represent weathered concrete. There is also a cinder covered fill approach. *CJ Riley*

**22**

This through truss bridge on the Boston & Maine is skewed by two panels, meaning the bridge sides are shifted laterally to compensate for the angle of the gap being crossed. *Historic American Engineering Record*

structural members on a bridge. Curved railroad bridges are made up of a series of short straight segments carefully positioned under the curving track, **21**. It is true that there may be examples of recent bridges, especially of concrete construction, that are built with a continuous curve, but it was computer-aided design that made the necessary complex calculations practicable. A railroad bridge with curved structural members won't be believable except in very rare contemporary situations.

Don't casually splice commercial bridge components together to create a longer span. There is a relatively fixed relationship between the depth of a beam and its allowable span. A bridge is a glorified beam, whether a girder or truss, and this relationship still rules. Most available models are in proper proportion. A longer span requires more structural depth to carry the same load, or else be much heavier. Adding a short length of plate girder to add, say, 10 percent to a span length would not raise alarms, but butting two full girders together isn't believable. Also, when butting plate girders, there are vertical stiffeners that are important structurally and there are usually more of them near the ends to counter bearing stresses.

If a "stretching" is necessary, shorten one girder and add a longer piece from the other, maintaining the spacing of these stiffeners. One could shorten a span to accommodate a heavier load or a double track, but be careful here and remove the piece from the middle. Any modification of bridge components must be done by even bays. A bay is a bridge segment that runs between vertical components (and the horizontal beams that connect the two sides).

Bridges should not be placed at an angle across a gap unless the bridge structure is "skewed," **22**. Extra span length costs extra money, so minimizing the span is good engineering. Skewing the bridge frame accomplishes this. As in the above, skewing is done in even bays for structural reasons.

## Bridge supports

The bearing ends of all bridge spans must be supported on substantial

**23**

The Western Maryland crossed Shaver's Fork of the Cheat River near Greenbrier Junction on a series of deck plate girders on tall concrete piers. The wing walls are composed of a well weathered tie cribbing of surprising height and there is a barely visible stone abutment. *CJ Riley*

bases (abutments at each end; piers for intermediate spans) that rest on solid ground, normally bedrock. We've all seen plastic models of through girder bridge that were just plopped on the ground (often a vertical dirt cliff) with the rails running over it. This is a major

affront to realism! The abutment both supports the bridge and retains the earthen approach fill that most bridges have. Moving dirt is cheaper than building a bridge span, so a fill is used as far as is practical.

The abutment (and often adjoining wing wall) can be as simple as a low structure of timbers installed sideways to begin a wooden trestle, **23**, or a more substantial concrete or stone structure that can be somewhat higher for a steel bridge.

Bridge ends don't simply rest on the abutments. Bearing ends are supported on pedestals (seats or shoes), **24**, devices that allow the bridge to expand and contract with temperature changes. One end will normally be on an anchored rocking device that allows minor changes in the bearing angle, **25**, and the other will be on a sliding bearing for the expansion. There are model castings available for these devices, and they are also included in better kits. It is also not difficult to to fabricate simple replicas in styrene; however they are made, a reasonable replica is critically important for realism.

On a multi-span bridge, each span must be supported by stone or concrete piers or steel or wood bents, as shown in several photos in this chapter. This is an area where so many well-intentioned modelers get it wrong. Each span is a separate structure

requiring appropriate bearings at the ends. There can be no intermediate support between the girder or truss ends. It's also inappropriate to connect the separate girders or trusses at a pier, since that would interfere with potential foundation settling and expansion/contraction with temperature changes.

## Culverts

To this point, we have been discussing the substantial bridges that highlight a model railroad, but we would be remiss in ignoring the lowly culvert, **26**. A culvert is very much a bridge, albeit a short one. A culvert, like its bigger brothers, can be of wood, stone, steel, or concrete construction, or—as Chapter 4 showed—even a simple pipe. It may span a small brook or, more commonly, carry drainage from a high side ditch under the roadbed to spill

**25**

This pin-connected truss was on a Pennsylvania RR branch near Canonsburg Pa. It nicely illustrates the heavier structural members that are in compression and the thin strip or rod material, which is in tension. The large pins that tie the connections together and simplify erection are clearly visible. This generally older method of building bridges allows the steel components to be prefabricated, minimizes riveting in the field, and maintains some flexibility. *CJ Riley*

**24**

The bearing plates under the girders are visible here, as is the builder's plate on the right girder. Note the extra angle stiffeners, the space between the girders which allows for expansion, and the well-weathered concrete. *CJ Riley*

down a hillside toward a stream.

It is often said by engineers that the three most important design considerations for a roadbed are drainage, drainage, and drainage. Good modeling will recognize this with proper ditches and regular culverts. I have a Western Maryland right-of-way diagram from a grade in the

**26**

**This very tall concrete and stone arch is on the Black Fork grade of the Western Maryland east of Elkins, West Virginia. My wife, at 5'-4", is dwarfed by the arch. We found debris apparently left by storm water high on the wing walls, illustrating the importance of culverts to protection of the roadbed.** *CJ Riley*

Alleghenies that indicates a culvert every 150 feet or so. There were many sizes and materials indicated but it was a clear indication of the importance of culverts.

Even in normally dry country, when it rains or snow melts, the water must go somewhere. Thus as modelers, we should pay close attention and include many culverts along our rail lines and roads. Culverts can be as simple as a steel pipe (soda straw or other tube), a pipe with a concrete headwall, a concrete box, a larger corrugated metal pipe, a stone arch (with side wing walls), a short wood trestle, or a simple bridge composed of a series of steel I-beams under the width of the rails. And a road that crosses the tracks will definitely have an appropriate culvert to carry the railroad's ditch water.

Bridges also carry roads and highways across railroads and streams, **27**, and those bridges should be just as carefully modeled as the ones carrying railways. The structural components of a road bridge will be lighter than a railroad bridge of equivalent span, but the various details still apply. Elevated road crossings may be the last holdout of timber framed bridges, **28**, therefore providing an opportunity for modelers with the trestle-building urge. Other types of wooden and simple steel beam bridges can be found supporting roads, and I have seen old flatcars recycled

**LEARNING POINTS ➡**

**1.** Select the proper type of bridge for the situation.

**2.** Provide proper piers and abutments along with appropriate bridge pedestals.

**3.** Only support bridges at the proper bearing points.

**4.** Skew the structure for angled crossings.

**5.** Culverts are also bridges and are much more common.

**6.** When laying track over a bridge (unless it's a ballasted deck), don't use ordinary sectional or flextrak on the girders. Use track designed for bridges, which has thicker ties placed closer together.

**7.** If kitbashing a bridge, remember that if the span is made longer the load limit will be reduced.

into bridges, especially on private drives.

Don't panic when faced with needing a bridge—keep the basic dos and don'ts in mind, and if in doubt, check prototype photos and refer to more-detailed books for further information. With some care, your bridges and culverts can be a highlight of your model railroad.

**27**

**Railroads also go under bridges, frequently those of roads. This is a very old cast iron pin-connected truss bridge near Sand Patch Pa.** *CJ Riley*

**28**

**Road overpasses built from wood can still be found in rural areas on secondary roads. This would be another way to satisfy the trestle-building bug.** *CJ Riley*

# CHAPTER SIX

# Modeling structures

While our trains should be the focus of attention, and scenery provides the setting for them, there would be little work for our modeled railroaders without structures to be served. Be it the local depot, **1**, large industries, or places for inhabitants to live and shop and visitors to stay, structures are important to creating a sense of place and reason for being.

**The B&O often built substantial brick depots in small towns along its original line to the Ohio River. One of the B&O's handsome mountain depots is at Oakland, Md. It was designed in the Queen Anne style by E. Francis Baldwin, architect for many of the railroad's more elegant depots.** *CJ Riley*

A depot is often the centerpiece of a town, but it is rare when a major urban terminal is the centerpiece of a model railroad. Dr. Nicholas Muff did so with his model of Kansas City's Union Station. This incredible model took several years to scratchbuild and has full interior detailing. His railroad was conceived to celebrate passenger trains and features the prototype train movements in the area of the station. *Nicholas Muff*

Older wood-framed elevators are fading away in favor of the less flammable corrugated metal silo designs. This grain elevator complex in Veedersburg, Ind., is a major presence in the town and replaced an earlier facility. *Tony Koester*

Entire books have been written about building and detailing structure models, so I'll stick to discussing other facets. I know many of us think first of building or assembling a village for our trains to serve—perhaps a holdover from the tinplate around the Christmas tree days—but we should approach the opportunities for various types of structures with a more open mind, taking advantage of the observation, understanding, and selection concepts previously discussed (see my comments in the Introduction).

## Be selective with structures

Once again, we need to go back to our prototypes, either specific or implied, to avoid randomly choosing structures for our railroads. Even if you are modeling from your favorite town, it is unlikely you can include *everything*, so an analysis of the most significant structures and their uses would be in order. When freelancing, it is still important to study a real location that represents your intentions so that your decisions reflect the prototype practices and appearance. Modeling from the

prototype remains the best approach for best results.

This analysis will determine the most important buildings, particularly those most directly related to the railroad. Other significant or landmark structures can also be "signature" items and should be carefully modeled, **2**. Signature industries might include a grain elevator, **3**, coal dealer, **4**, or perhaps a large manufacturing plant. Depots, **5**, freight houses, signal towers, or perhaps even the local crossing shanty may be critical to

Coal dealers were once common to almost every town and could be of a wide variety of designs. The basic concept was an elevator to raise the coal into the bins according to size and a chute system to transfer the coal to trucks. Some dumped from a trestle and loaded trucks with a portable conveyor. *CJ Riley*

The Baltimore & Ohio built many frame depots to a standard design at lesser locations, such as this one at Rowlesburg, W.Va. It's typical of small-town depots found across the U.S. Railroads often created a standard station design with multiple size options to suit towns of varying sizes. *CJ Riley*

**6** Railroads often run through the back yards of towns. This is the B&O in Sistersville, W.Va. Details include the wooden road crossing, the sidewalks across the tracks, the cabinets and equipment for the crossing signals, the hedge along the road that turns to follow the tracks, and that most houses are painted white. *CJ Riley*

**7** Business areas also back up to the tracks. The Pennsylvania's main line was depressed for running through several Pittsburgh neighborhoods including East Liberty. The streets all cross on through girder bridges; there are non-matching stone retaining walls between the abutments and there's a great deal of trash. *CJ Riley*

making a town recognizable. Non-signature buildings such as common storefronts or houses might be more easily represented by "stand-in" models that are similar in style, but not exact replicas—but even there, signs from the prototype will help cement the illusion.

The hobby is blessed with hundreds of structure kits, from simple plastic to complex craftsman styles. They cover a range of building styles from old to modern, and from large industrial complexes to small structures. Choose structures carefully, as they set the tone for believablility, both in terms of being appropriate for a particular region, railroad, or era, and for being realistic models.

Take a good look at what railroad and industrial structures remain in the real world and it will be obvious that they are rather plain. Older brick buildings may have arches over the windows and some decorative brick patterns, and there are occasional well-designed depots featuring complex designs, but you will rarely find cantilevers, multiple roof lines running amok at steep angles, or dormers in impossibly tiny attic spaces—which unfortunately can be found on many models.

The lesson is to avoid model structures that are overly complex, cartoonish, or cutesy. Modeling from the prototype means eschewing such

**8** A cluster of buildings—a store, gas station, implement dealer, and feed mill—are all that is needed to signify a town at this crossing. The wonderful backdrop certainly adds to the illusion, but even if parallel to the tracks, these structures would signify a town in farm country. It could be easily assumed the rest of the town was behind the photographer. *Tom Johnson*

models in favor of those that match what the prototype did (or would have done).

It's common for the railroad to pass through the backyards of towns, **6**, and I have always been a fan of modeling towns in that manner. Therefore, think about including the backs of commercial buildings, **7**, businesses such as welding and auto repair shops, industries of all kinds, laundry on the line behind a house, a car up on blocks, and a thousand other details. Except in smaller towns, the areas around the railroad are rarely the best neighborhoods, except maybe near

the depot, **5**. In truth, I avoid much modeling of non-railroad businesses, preferring to emphasize the industries and relegating the town to a few representative structures with the rest of the town on the backdrop or just implied. This allows for maximum use of our layouts' limited spaces.

Many towns have a depot square, and with the depot placed to the rear of the tracks, a simple backdrop of commercial storefronts (flats or shallow relief) set along "Railroad Avenue" can imply much more town than is modeled. If the depot is placed on the near (aisle) side, the "other side of the

**9**

Coaling towers and docks were located at key points along railroad lines through the steam era. Large concrete docks were common at important terminals as at Grafton. Some still stand, unused, due to demolition difficulties. *CJ Riley*

tracks" is fertile ground for background structures such as the rear walls of commercial buildings or industries that would be common there in the real world.

You can fit enough of a town on even a narrow shelf, **8**, to imply that there's more of the town nearby by using key structures in the foreground with building flats and partial buildings. See Chapter 2 for more details on these techniques.

Railroad service structures and buildings can also be signature items, including steam-era coaling towers, **9**, and water tanks, **10**. Don't forget interlocking towers, **11**, and other details such as loading platforms at team tracks, often found near depots, **12**.

Even when modeling a larger city scene, much of the city can be implied, since railroads rarely run through the heart of downtown. A few of the smaller "edge of downtown" buildings near the depot could be modeled, with the major structures as cutouts

glued to the backdrop. For an urban switching layout, massive industrial and commercial structures along the tracks would dominate, again with the taller downtown on the backdrop. Depending on era, structure roofs may include water tanks, enclosures for elevator hoists, air-conditioning units, piping and other mechanical equipment, along with stairwell enclosures.

Painted wall signs were common (and still are), but that is a detail frequently overdone on models. Keep signs appropriate to eras. Painted signs of bygone products and eras should appear old and faded. This is another area where it's better to model what is typical rather than the unusual, unless the unusual item is a signature element that helps identify the locale.

## Plausible industries

In most prototype urban locations, industrial structures usually dominate the areas along the tracks. It follows that it should be that way in our

**10**

The Chesapeake & Ohio's Thurmond, W.Va., engine water facility, left, included both a tower and a ground-mounted tank with a pump house (water was provided to locomotives via standpipes and to numerous railroad buildings). An advantage of modeling from the prototype is the opportunity to model a scene correctly and therefore realistically, rather than guessing about it. At right is my model of the Thurmond tanks. *Two photos: CJ Riley*

**11** Interlocking towers controlled turnouts and signals at crossings, junctions, and crossovers. They were common through the late 1900s. This Baltimore & Ohio tower, at a long-forgotten location, is typical of those of many railroads. *CJ Riley*

**12** Team tracks are sidings or spurs with gravel or pavement adjacent and enough room for truck access, allowing rail access for businesses located away from the tracks. Team tracks were often located near depots, and car-deck-level ramps like this one were common. The background retail buildings are mostly unadorned, simple facades. *CJ Riley*

modeling as well. Many railroads (or cities or regions) have a dominant industry, and it's logical for models relating to that industry to be prevalent.

For example, coal is a common modeling theme since coal was the reason for the construction of many railroad lines (especially in the east). Although coal mining and traffic have evolved, coal is still a key revenue source and is still critical for many industrial processes as well as power generation. Likewise, grain and other agricultural traffic dominate railroads in the granger areas and plains states. Other railroads have been (and are) keyed on other industries, including lumber, produce, chemicals, or oil. Let your prototype be your guide.

Don't despair if your layout doesn't have sufficient space for a large industry that may be a signature item. It's possible to include large industries by modeling all or most on the backdrop (using flats, photos, or a combination), or with short lengths of track leading toward the structure through the foreground trees. With enough track, operations are possible in a small space.

Also think about the structures and/or products related to your main

**13** The Monte Christo concentrator in Washington state was built to process gold deposits from the Cascade Mountains. The rail line carried the bounty to the Puget Sound city of **Everett.** *Di Voss collection*

**14** The Christo concentrator is featured on Didrick Voss's **Everett & Monte Christo Railroad, and is a great example of modeling from a prototype. Di was able to find adequate historical material to accurately model locomotives, rolling stock, and structures.** *Di Voss*

Small feed mills and stores are staples of towns across the plains and wherever animals are raised. Unlike elevators, they received loads by rail instead of generating them. *CJ Riley*

For most of us, a series of smaller rail-served industries (such as Gauley Feeds) that can be modeled completely works better than fewer, larger industries. *CJ Riley*

industries, **13**, **14**. For example, coal mines often mean company towns, company stores, union halls, machinery repair companies, and so on. A town on the great plains inevitably includes grain elevators, an implement dealer,

stock pens, and a feed store, **15**, **16**. These logical clusters will add greatly to the sense of rightness, as will common buildings such as gas stations, taverns, diners, and repair shops, all of which are often found near the tracks. Oil or

propane dealers, coal yards and other businesses that receive goods should also be represented, as they will add to operations.

I haven't said much about houses because personally I see modeling a village as wasting space that could be used to provide operating interest, **17**, **18**. A cluster of company houses along the tracks might be an exception, or an occasional farm house and barn, **19**, but houses in a town can be implied rather than modeled. It can be of great advantage to place these secondary structures in the background and by building them to a slightly smaller scale, take advantage of forced perspective to increase the apparent depth of a scene. This illusion can be helped with smaller scale figures and vehicles.

It's easy to make grand plans for layouts, not fully considering how much time it will take to build and model all of it. We all need to make judicious use of our modeling time, particularly with secondary or background models, **20**. It is better to focus detailing time on significant (foreground) industries and structures. It is also true that many fine but small craftsman kits seem to be too expensive to casually purchase. However, it is possible reduce the costs of such kits by using the components for two structures.

I first did that with a beautiful Thomas Yorke cast plaster structure by using the front wall and one side

Company towns were typically built by mining and mill companies in remote areas. They featured simple construction, and houses were often packed tightly together.

For my company-housing town, I built these rough duplexes from styrene at a scale of .10" to the foot, just under HO scale. They look fine from a distance, but up close you can see the doors and windows were drawn on with black ink and only two walls were built for each house. Buried in the trees, they hint at what must be present all over the hill. *CJ Riley*

**19**

Among the most iconic American images is the red barn. Since barn styles are regional, it's best to match a barn to the area modeled. Paul Dolkos built this background barn model to a smaller scale to force the perspective and make it appear more distant. *Paul Dolkos*

for a structure facing the aisle and the rear wall casting and other side for a building across the street whose back faces the aisle. It seemed terribly wasteful to put that beautifully carved brickwork where it couldn't be seen, **21**. I substituted plain styrene walls for those not visible and it worked so effectively that I now do it regularly, even on scratchbuilt models, if they are not destined for a contest. It is far

better use of modeling time to focus on what is visible since the observer's eye will assume that the whole model is fully detailed.

If there is only a slight view of a side wall due to the angle of placement, a plain wall painted to match will often suffice if obscured by a well-detailed tree, billboard or other feature. Save that side and the rear for another location. If adjacent structures abut or

have a narrow walkway between them, you can save two walls with no loss of realism.

Similarly, a structure placed against a mirror will double its apparent size, a technique particularly valuable for very large structures or a repetitive configuration such as a long bank of coke ovens. Once again, a lot of modeling time can be saved and perhaps additional space made available

**20**

It makes the best use of our modeling time to focus detailing efforts on foreground structures and models. Buildings in the background can be simpler and less detailed. *CJ Riley*

**21**

The brick building at left was an expensive cast plaster kit, but I replaced the rear and side walls (also on the adjacent styrene buildings)—which wouldn't be seen here—with blank styrene walls. These components were used as the sides and rears of structures across the street. *CJ Riley*

**22** Even basic plastic kits can be easily upgraded for more realism as with this ancient Atlas water tank model. A paint job is critical to eliminate the plastic shine and provide a sense of aging. Real chain was added on the spout and heavier weights were added so the spout can operate. *CJ Riley*

**23** Little white churches are found in small towns and rural areas all over Appalachia and in many other areas. One doesn't need an elaborate church in most small towns, but the setting is important. This is the Beverly Presbyterian Church in Beverly, W.Va. *Carol M. Highsmith, Library of Congress*

for another industry. See Chapter 4 for more on mirrors.

Many modelers steer clear of scratchbuilding (or even building complex kits) because of a perceived lack of personal skills. I contend that model-building skills can be learned by almost anyone who tries. However, even if you elect to stick with the simpler styrene kits it is possible to produce outstanding models by adding paint and additional details, **22**. This might mean certain prototypes are beyond your grasp, but reasonable substitutes can often be had with some creative kitbashing.

When using common styrene kits, avoid building them straight out of the box. At a minimum, paint all the parts. For brick buildings, highlight individual bricks with nearly matching paint or artists' pens to create a little variation and texture. A number of paints and other products are available for simulating mortar joints.

Do as much painting and detailing as possible before assembling the walls.

It is much easier to paint, add mortar, apply signs, weather the walls and seal with flat spray (before glazing and window curtains are applied) when the components are flat on a workbench. Doing this extra work goes a long way to transform your kit into something more believable than a raw plastic assembly.

Combining kits or using modular wall components for larger structures is also effective modeling. With a little experience, more complicated kitbashing, craftsman kits, and even scratchbuilding could be in your future.

A small community is not complete without its iconic white church, **23**, general store, and gas station, nor is an urban neighborhood complete without its corner store. Another consideration would be other signature structures such as retail chain stores and fast food places, which have progressed with the eras. Make sure you keep these branded stores appropriate for the period modeled—remember K-Mart was once Kresge's and McDonald's were little walk-up boxes under the golden arches.

Also remember icons like orange juice stands, gas stations in a coffee pot, diners converted from old trolley cars, and many more. Only include them if appropriate, but little details like this draw observers into the scene and allow most of the rest to be less important in the background.

## LEARNING POINTS ➔

**1.** Focus on signature structures.

**2.** Railroads often run through the backyards of towns.

**3.** Think about structures related to your industries.

**4.** It is sometimes not necessary to finish all four walls.

**5.** Don't be afraid to kitbash or scratchbuild structures when advantageous.

**6.** Expensive kits may be justified by using some walls for other projects.

**7.** Assemble and detail walls flat on the workbench before final assembly.

1

# CHAPTER SEVEN

# Weathering

The great John Allen amazed the model railroad world in 1948 when he began to publish photos of rolling stock and structure models that showed the effects of passing time and the elements on his models. Those techniques became known as weathering, **1**, and considerable controversy was generated at the time over the appropriateness of these techniques, **2**.

Weathering is a key to realism. I built Pochahontas Coal from scribed wood siding, with the wood slightly distressed and stained lightly with gray. Individual boards were then restained with the blue or a weathered gray. Further aging was done with powdered chalks, then the sign was made with dry transfers that were lightly sanded for fading and wear.
*CJ Riley*

**2**

John Allen was a pioneer in weathering. John scratchbuilt this stock car for his narrow gauge Devil's Gulch & Helengon in swaybacked fashion and heavily weathered it, with a redolent mixture of straw bedding and bovine residue visible through the open door. *John Allen*

**3**

These Santa Fe locomotives are not shiny black, but heavily weathered and stained gray. White stains from impurities and chemicals in the water streak down from the whistle and safety valves as well as near the blowdown cocks under the cabs. The canvas cab weather curtains are dark and dirty and there is a coating of dust on each tender, along with black streaks from spilled fuel oil. The concrete coaling tower is sooty black, but there are lighter stains from sand as well. The rails are shiny on top, but rusty on the sides. *Jack Delano, Library of Congress*

There was considerable reverence at that time for models with beautiful high-gloss finishes, sometimes painted with samples obtained from actual railroad shops so that the colors were "perfect." Unfortunately, as John pointed out, these beautiful finishes did not really replicate the prototype. How could this be, you might ask? After all, it was painted with the real paint.

There are many factors at work here. First, daylight (especially direct sunlight) is many times brighter than indoor light. The color temperature is different as well, with natural and artificial light having varying amounts of different colors (and the many types of indoor light varying in color temperature as well). Outdoors, the

atmosphere affects color, especially for objects viewed at extreme distances; the size of a real locomotive also changes color perception compared to seeing a small model.

All of this means that a fresh, glossy finish on a new prototype locomotive simply does not "scale down" (for want of a better phrase) in miniature. Colors generally appear darker inside, and the hue will be affected by whatever artificial light is used, so even a model representing a freshly shopped prototype will not look right. See

Chapter 8 for more discussion of color.

One way to explain this is to think about the older generation of photographers who worked hard to shoot black steam locos early or late in the day. With the slow speed black & white film available, having a low sun shining directly on the side of the locomotive brought out all the black detail that would have been in dark shadows under a noon sun, thus all but invisible. These steam locos then looked grayer than they might have been and there were stains from steam

**4**

This Chesapeake & Ohio SD40-2 shows several weathering patterns. The dark blue paint is somewhat faded and the black trucks and fuel tanks have faded to dark gray. Grilles and louvers attract grime, as does the pilot. The front of the fuel tank has picked up a lot of dirt from the right-of-way and there is an oily stain below the fuel filler. The yellow stripe along the frame is almost obscured. *John Roberts*

**5**

Wooden structures provide a good chance to test various finishing skills. Hinerman Brothers exhibits a range of possibilities, from simple faded paint to peeling and failing paint and a higher-quality finish around the storefront. *CJ Riley*

An overview of the Milwaukee Road yard in Bensenville Ill., in 1943, shows a wide range of colors, fading, and weathering that affect freight cars. There are a few new-looking cars, a car at the rear (right) with a steel door that doesn't match its wood sides, a mix of dirty and clean reefers, and chalk markings on many cars. *Jack Delano, Library of Congress*

leaks at fittings, dirt blown up from the roadbed, wayward lubrication, soot, and general fading from the sun as well as regular high-pressure steam cleaning, **3**. Diesels, **4**, rolling stock, and structures, **5**, suffer similarly.

Aging begins with paint failure. Ultraviolet rays, temperature changes, rain, and snow all contribute to the phenomenon called "chalking," particularly with older paints. The outer "skin" of the paint literally dissolves over time, washing down the surface in the rain and taking any high gloss with it. White lettering on rolling stock is easily seen to streak softly down below as it dissolves, but all colors do this somewhat as can be seen by the visible fading of bright hues on modern era

freight cars. Colors will become duller and change hues as paint finishes age.

Spilled lading, soot from steam locos, oily exhaust from diesels, damaged paint that exposes the steel to rust, and other environmental exposures all contribute to the aging process, **6**. And don't forget, cast steel components such as wheels and couplers are normally left unpainted to not hide cracks that could predict a failure. When new cars and locomotives emerge from the shop, they normally have rusty wheels and couplers. In the steam era, rusty wheels quickly became very greasy and caked with dirt due to lube oil leaking from the journal boxes, but wheels in modern roller bearings tend to stay

rusty and/or dirty.

There are many methods for effectively reproducing these various effects. Washes of oil or water-based paints, powdered pigments, weathering powders, facial makeup, drybrushing, airbrushing, and alcohol misting all have a place in the modeler's repertoire, They can all work well—each modeler generally develops a preference for specific techniques. Whichever you choose to use, work to master them for a proper variety in weathering appearance. After all, each piece of equipment has passed through different environments over differing amounts of time so the weathering should vary accordingly, **7**, **8**.

Structures may stay in one place, but

A resin model of a Pennsy car modified with a raised roof for shipment of Jeeps during WWII is supposed to be almost new, so the weathering is light, but there are numerous chalk marks including a "Kilroy" graffiti done with a sharpened china pencil. *CJ Riley*

Appropriate weathering, copied from a prototype photo, illustrates how realistic a model can be. The washed-out cement stains were done with several applications of thinned paint. There are paint patches where data was revised, a placard on the left-end tack board, and chalk marks. *Richard Hendrickson*

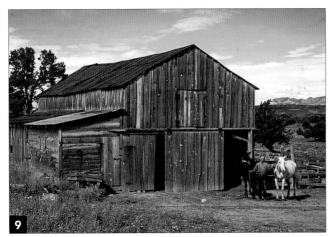

**9**

Bill Stagg, homesteader, poses in front of his barn in Pie Town, N.M., in October 1940. This unpainted wood barn shows typical aging patterns, with knots that stand out as different colors. The metal roofing exhibits deep rusting and a dark color (except for a more recent repair), and dirt has splashed up on the lower part of the door. Also notice what is missing: visible nail holes, an often-overdone model builder's fancy. *Russell Lee, Library of Congress*

**10**

This cut-stone retaining wall, supporting former Pennsy tracks in Pittsburgh, still shows effects of heavy exposure to coal smoke and soot 50 years after clean air acts took place. The wall allows the tracks to be elevated while running next to the neighboring sidewalk and street in the foreground. *Larry Kline*

**11**

Krider Coal, another retail dealership, was built with individually stained boards that provide a natural variation among them. The faded sign was made with dry transfer lettering on a thinly painted white background, then sanded. The weathering reflects the splashed-up coal dust at the bottoms of the silos, with moisture wicking up the siding. *CJ Riley*

they age just the same, **9**. The sun fades and chalks paint, paint peels away, grime accumulates, gutters leak (and that water can cause stains), boards warp (and break and pull away from structures), shingles fall off, windows break (and are sometimes boarded up), rain splashes up on foundations and washes dirt down walls, leaving traces.

Remember that up into the 1950s, coal smoke dominated much of America. Steam locomotives, home and business furnaces, various industrial processes, and power plants spewed huge amounts of pollutants into the air, and these fumes and soot also impacted structures.

I spent many years in Pittsburgh beginning 10 years after the city's clean air movement began. Beautiful brick, stone and terra cotta structures emerged from under heavy black coatings of soot. One of the exceptions were the many massive stone retaining walls along both railroads and highways: these surfaces weren't deemed worthy of cleaning and thus remained black some 40 years later, **10**.

I also noticed this condition when hiking along rural Baltimore & Ohio tracks. Even in very remote areas, the soot and sulphur fumes from passing steam locomotives stained all stone black, including tunnel portals, retaining walls, and exposed rock outcroppings. However, I have seen clean stone bridge abutments on the former Delaware, Lackawanna &

**12**

Individually colored bricks can provide a subtle weathering effect, as on this building. The light gray bricks (near the eaves), painted in diamond patterns, imitate decorative effects often used on prototype brick buildings. *CJ Riley*

Hemlock Mines' siding was pre-stained gray, then cut to length and assembled on a strip of masking tape. The area behind the lettering was stained with a thin white, then the dry transfer lettering was applied and the streaky red stain applied overall. The dry transfers were lifted off with masking tape, leaving white lettering. Further streaking of boards with darker gray added to the aging. A lot of powdered charcoal was splashed around the lower areas and the coal chutes. *CJ Riley*

Gondola interiors take a fearsome beating. Wooden decks get chewed up by fasteners holding bracing, the paint is scraped by loads, and they are rarely properly cleaned out, leaving the detritus from previous loads or trash that has been dumped. *Dick Flock*

Western that showed no signs of this staining. Was it because of the cleaner-burning anthracite coal used on that railroad and in nearby buildings? Or might they have been cleaned?

I honestly don't know, but they provide the lesson that one should be careful when coloring stonework and adding other weathering effects on a model. Examine the prototype in your modeled area in person or in photos before applying elaborate stains and variations of natural stone or brick colors near the right of way. A sooty coating may be more appropriate in your area or era.

## Modeling effects

This chapter isn't meant to be a how-to explanation of the various weathering techniques. There have been countless magazine articles, books, and online sources with detailed instructions. Try the various methods to see what works for you, and practice them a few times to become proficient.

Weathering or aging begins with the original surface of the model, **11, 12**. It doesn't matter what material you're starting with: Wood, styrene, metal, cardstock, resin castings—they

are all useful and can be adapted to represent multiple prototype materials, although perhaps not equally effectively. Whatever the material, the initial work you do pays dividends during the finishing. As an example, many modelers think that only wood can represent wood, but that is not true. Even fine basswood grain is way out of scale for modeling. However, if it is aged, unpainted wood you want, wood is a good start, although styrene can be used very effectively without the over-scale grain.

I am firmly convinced that it's the basic texture of the modeling material that makes the finish look good, **13**. Thus, a naturally smooth material such as styrene or brass represents metal well, but if you want styrene to look like wood, it must have a texture somewhat like wood. I'm not a fan of styrene (or wood) that's been excessively carved and scraped to simulate oversized grain, but it is a style that some can carry off. Remember, we are viewing our models from a considerable scale distance (typically 100 or more scale feet in HO) and real wood grain disappears very quickly. It's not the distinct individual grain

that we see, but a subtle texture that is easily noticed as different from metal, for example.

I like to give styrene a "tooth" by lightly sanding it with moderate grit sandpaper, painting it lightly, and then using a powdered material to reduce any sheen. Wood often needs light sanding to remove leftover fuzz, and pre-staining before assembly can improve a final finish, particularly if heavier weathering is to be depicted. I feel nothing represents chalking paint better than a powdered material rubbed into the surface early in the process. Other wet finishes can follow if the powder is sealed. Even if it appears the material has disappeared, it has still left a soft finish like chalking paint.

In addition to natural aging, human activities contribute to the sense of passing time. Flat car decks and gondola and boxcar floors become chewed up with damage caused by loading and unloading. The loads often leave evidence. Nails, bolts, blocking, and tie-downs used to secure loads leave marks in their wakes, **14**, and

**15**

Hopper car interiors also take a beating from their loads. Here, iron ore is being loaded at the Pennsylvania's Cleveland ore docks in 1943. Car interior colors vary considerably: newer cars still have some paint left, and the rust varies from bright orange to dark brown. *Jack Delano, Library of Congress*

**16**

Tank cars also suffer from loading spills. This modern GATX car exhibits considerable staining, likely from an acidic material. *CJ Riley*

this blocking and other packaging are often left in empty cars and visible in operation.

Gondola sides can become bent and bulged from heavy loads banging into them. Wet coal creates acids that eat through slope sheet joints in hopper cars, **15**, and older hoppers may have wads of rags or paper stuffed in the gaps to prevent leakage. Boxcars or covered hoppers loaded with cement, either bagged or bulk, will show stains and textures from this caustic material, and loose grain will collect near the hatches of grain cars. Many tank cars, **16**, show lading stains from various chemicals, spilled oil or tar, yellow sulphur, or lighter stains from gasoline or diesel fuel mixed with dust. The point is obvious: Consider the lading when modeling the effects of age and weather.

Railroad workers applied chalk markings to cars as part of the sorting and delivery process, **17**. Old marks might be scratched out to avoid confusion and new marks might be in a variety of locations or colors appropriate to the work being done, **18**. Additionally, there might be routing cards or other small pieces of paper stapled to the tack boards on the cars. Cars carrying hazardous materials are also appropriately placarded as a warning to workers (and these placards

**17**

Through the 1960s, car routing and spotting information was often chalked on car sides by agents and train crews. *Library of Congress*

**18**

This view shows the dented sides typical of older gondolas and a variety of chalk marks, with some older notes crossed out.

**19**

Weathering on this boxcar includes lots of decal chalk marks as well as repainted and restenciled load limit and light weight information. *Richard Hendrickson*

## LEARNING POINTS →

**1.** Everything begins to age as soon as it's built.

**2.** Paint chalking occurs very quickly outdoors.

**3.** Rot in wood and rust on steel occur very quickly after paint failure.

**4.** Wheels and couplers are normally unpainted.

**5.** Dirt and rust stains run vertically from their origins.

**6.** Some paint failures are caused by accidental scrapes or repeated rubbing.

**7.** A variety of aging techniques and materials provide the best realism.

**8.** Weathering should properly reflect the passage of time, with newer items weathered less than older ones, unless they have been repainted.

**9.** Railroad workers get very dirty, but even your model citizens need to have their coloring toned down and flattened. Emphasize clothing creases and facial features with colored pencils.

**20**

Large, colorful graffiti has become all too common on modern locomotives and freight cars. Some modelers choose to replicate the elaborate designs on their models; others choose to ignore it.

**21**

A PFM brass model of a Russian Decapod has been finished with a grayed-out black and weathered with washes and powered colors. Note the stain on the rear of the tender caused by overflowing water cascading down the side. Kanawha no. 1018 has the look of a well-used but well-maintained engine. *CJ Riley*

have changed greatly from the steam era to today).

These markings can be duplicated with decals (Sunshine Models once offered several sheets of markings; Microscale and others offer them as parts of several decal sets), **19**. They can also be re-created with artist's pencils, fine-point wax pencils, or gel pens.

Finally, there's the issue of graffiti, **20**. It's almost impossible to watch a freight train pass without seeing large, colorful graffiti that takes up most (or all) of multiple freight car sides (not to mention locomotives). Large areas of graffiti are also common in many metro areas on structures, bridges, and retaining walls.

My general sense is that most modelers feel the early simple markings, like "Herbie," are charming, but that modern spray-painted graffiti should not be duplicated. You're welcome to your opinion, but I feel strongly that, although distasteful, this graffiti is a prominent feature of the modern world and on a model railroad, graffiti is part of a realistic rendition of this era. This all falls into the area of "cultural texture," the often-subtle bits of information that, along with local details, signs, and product advertising, add to the ambiance of what is being represented.

Over the years, I have seen many model railroads with fine rolling stock,

handsome structures, and impressive scenery, that still failed to draw me in. I found the key, almost always, was a lack of a sense of passing time. All the structures were pristine and the locomotives and cars sparkling new, as if they were in a museum or a part of Disneyland. Yes, it is possible to go too far in the other direction, with everything run down and decrepit, but a well-balanced model railroad exhibits a sense of being a small slice of the real world, warts and all. Showing signs of history and passing time with a variety of weathering techniques and levels of aging help to set the models in context and are major contributors to that elusive sense of rightness, **21**.

# The importance of color

On a sunny day in June 1964, this brand-new Santa Fe 86-foot auto parts car appears bright red and the neighboring Wabash car is a deep, dark blue. On a cloudy day, however, the red will appear muted and not as bright, and the dark blue will appear almost black. As the cars age, the color shades will change as paint oxidizes and grime and dirt coat the car. *John S. Ingles; J. David Ingles collection*

I've touched on the subject of color in previous chapters, but there's more to this complex subject worth further exploration. Color can stir up many arguments (such as what exactly the "proper" match is for such-and-such railroad's paint schemes), **1**, and failing to accurately capture colors—whether on equipment or in nature—can kill the realism of a scene or an entire layout.

## Perceptions

We must first understand that individuals perceive colors differently (without even getting into color blindness). Color appearance changes considerably in different types of light—this effect is measurable as color temperature. For example, outdoor light has more blue than most indoor lighting, but outdoor light varies by time of day (light near sunrise and sunset has more reds). Clouds and atmospheric conditions also affect color perception.

Indoor (artificial) light varies considerably: incandescent bulbs make colors appear warmer and redder; most fluorescent lights will make colors seem cooler or greener (but tubes vary widely); LED and halogen bulbs provide a still different light and therefore affect the appearance of color. Also keep in mind that color reproduction in photographic prints, on the printed page, and on computer monitors may also vary considerably from the original image.

It isn't the color that changes. The actual color is determined by the pigments and other ingredients of paint (and other materials). The light determines how our eyes (and brains) perceive the color. So if it was important to precisely match a prototype color by finding a paint chip or mixture that is indistinguishable when holding it against the color to be matched, that would be just the beginning. The change in appearance from the original light to the light used to illuminate the model will need to be considered.

As an example: If you painted an HO boxcar with the same dark blue paint as used on the Wabash boxcar in **1**, and held it outside in the same bright sunlight, you'd be very happy with the color. However, when you brought that car inside and placed it on your layout under relatively dim (compared to direct sunlight) incandescent bulbs, you would be disappointed to see that it looks black. Then, when you brought it to your workbench and held it directly under a bright light bulb, you would be disappointed again as the blue might

**2**

Western Maryland No. 6 pulls a freight on the Cass Scenic Railroad in West Virginia. While the freshly painted locomotive looks terrific, the detail is completely lost in the glossy, pitch-black paint. *CJ Riley*

**3**

Even on this well-maintained museum piece (Cass Scenic Heisler no. 6), the paint is several years old and has weathered to dark gray. The detail is much easier to see, but there is still a slight gloss. A model painted like this would look right even indoors in artificial light. *CJ Riley*

**4**

There are several shades visible on these model Union Pacific steamers being fueled and watered. None are black, yet they all look correct as our eyes accept them as black. Painting like this represents the passage of time since each locomotive has been out of the shops a different amount of time. *Mike Brock*

take on a slightly purple tone (from the red shift caused by the bulb).

Another fundamental tenet is that black and other dark colors hide detail, **2**. Freshly painted steam locomotives were gloss black, but—because black

and other dark colors absorb light—it's almost impossible at times to see shadows and intricate features on their surfaces. This obviously also applies to black and dark blue diesels and freight cars as well. It's not until these items start to weather and fade, **3**, that details begin to emerge. The lesson to take in modeling is to paint our models in lighter shades, **4**, to account for these factors.

If that weren't complicated enough, standard freight car, locomotive, and structure colors will vary even on

5

The Chicago & North Western boxcars in the three rows closest to the camera are all relatively clean, but there is considerable variation in the shades of the standard "freight car brown." The cars farther to the rear show quite a variation in the dirt and weathering that affects the apparent colors, even though they are from the same railroad. *Jack Delano, Library of Congress*

6

Modern paints may hold up better than those of the steam era, but the removable hoods on these coil steel cars still suffer from fading, loss of gloss, surface failure, dirt, and rust. *John Roberts*

7

This scene in World War II-era Chicago illustrates the wide variety of colors on vehicles at the time, including both the trucks and autos, and the muted colors of the brick building in the background. Note also the varied colors and shades of the gravel parking lot. *Jack Delano, Library of Congress*

the prototype, **5**. In the steam era, it was common for different railroad shops to mix their own paints from standard recipes. If the locally available iron oxide pigment varied, so did the shading of the paint. Some railroads ordered paint from multiple paint manufacturers—these could vary as well (or be a perfect match under one type of light, but quite dissimilar under other types of light). Era can also be a factor, if railroads and paint manufacturers changed paint ingredients or color specifications.

Add the effects of fading from the sun, discoloration from smoke and other air pollution, and rust, and the colors vary even more, **6**. Then there's the problem of atmospheric distortion. A real-world distance of one foot is the HO equivalent of 87 feet, so normal model viewing distance could easily scale out to a couple of hundred feet or more of air (moisture, haze, and pollution) between a viewer and amodel, **7**. When you also factor the difference in brightness between outdoors and indoors the model will seem darker.

So, what's a modeler to do?

It is not unreasonable to establish the prototype color as closely as

possible, but use that as a starting point to lighten it, gray it, dirty it, and fade it. Only you can decide how precisely you want to match a color. My personal approach is to determine if, for example, a "boxcar red" boxcar has a shade that's reddish brown, a brownish red, just brown, or some other shade.

Structures also require research and an understanding of color history. During the Victorian era, frame buildings were painted in brighter colors with contrasting trim, **8**. Craftsman era houses used earth tones with muted colors on trim, commonly green or maroon, which are also common on the windows and doors of brick buildings. But during the most

commonly modeled eras, white frame houses with dark green trim were the norm, **9**. You might see some black or dark blue occasionally but white and green dominated until post-World War II aluminum siding destroyed the character of countless homes, making them all white, and that may be important data for your own era. In more modern times, the beiges and grays with white trim came into prominence.

Remember, also, that most brick is not actually red! Painted brick might be red, but natural brick is normally a muted shade of orange (terra cotta), **10**. Brickworks were once located in every area of the country, so most brick

Victorian houses were known for the elaborate multi-color paint schemes that brought out the details in the ornamentation, though these specific colors could also represent the craftsman era. *Carol M. Highsmith, Library of Congress*

By the 1950s, white siding dominated the housing of America, even as many houses were re-clad in aluminum siding. If there was a contrasting trim color, it would likely be green or blue. *CJ Riley*

The brick on the left is somewhat orange (terra cotta) while the brick to the right is darker. Note the slight texture caused by variations in the brick color that occur during firing. While there is mortar, it is not white and blends somewhat with the brick. The edge of the building at far left is not stone but textured concrete block designed to resemble cut stone and a common way to save costs. *CJ Riley*

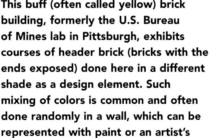

This buff (often called yellow) brick building, formerly the U.S. Bureau of Mines lab in Pittsburgh, exhibits courses of header brick (bricks with the ends exposed) done here in a different shade as a design element. Such mixing of colors is common and often done randomly in a wall, which can be represented with paint or an artist's pen to highlight individual bricks. *CJ Riley*

Structural clay tile was sometimes used instead of brick as its larger size required less labor. More commonly used in interior walls for fireproof construction, glazed tile could be found on exteriors, particularly barns, silos and industrial buildings. The windows were sized to match the grid of the tiles. *CJ Riley*

buildings would reflect the colors of the local clays, although there were additives that could modify the clay color. In some areas, dark brown would dominate, or cream, **11**, terra cotta, brownish red, or yellow. It was expensive to ship a low-value product such as brick a long distance, so local colors would be most common. Brick might also be glazed (like tile) in any conceivable color, **12**, but glazed brick

was more expensive and most-often found on commercial buildings.

The apparent color of brick is also somewhat dependent on the color of the mortar joints. While the mortar only makes up a small percentage of the wall, it's enough to affect how we perceive overall brick color. Normal mortar color is medium gray, but it can vary from almost white (rare) to dark gray. Also, mortar is often tinted to

make it closer to the color of the bricks being used. Again, look at prototype examples before modeling.

When modeling the steam era, we sometimes have to make educated guesses on colors when modeling from black & white photos. I once began construction of an elaborate freelanced coal preparation plant and tipple based on several photos. I started with a sky blue, **13**, since I had noticed that

**13**

Test-fitting this partially completed coal prep plant showed me a major error in the color choice. The bright sky blue color jumps into view, looming over the ridge intended to separate and isolate two scenes. *CJ Riley*

**14**

Repainting the prep plant a medium green settled the structure more naturally into the scenery. The building now works well in the background and doesn't grab immediate attention. *CJ Riley*

color on many prototype corrugated metal buildings. Fortunately, I set the uncompleted building in its location while working on other projects and happened to take a photo of the adjacent scene. The sky-blue tipple loomed over the hillside and just looked wrong. I quickly realized that although blue was a common color on more modern industrial buildings, it was perhaps not appropriate for the World War II era I was modeling. A

coat of medium green paint and all was well, **14**. The tipple blended into the hill. Lesson learned: Don't jump to quick conclusions regarding color and don't be afraid to change.

## The obvious isn't always obvious

We sometimes make false assumptions about colors based on generalities without really looking at specific examples. Good examples are common paving materials: Concrete is not gray and asphalt is not black! Yes, when freshly laid, asphalt is nearly black and

concrete is a very light gray (nearly white). However, both quickly weather, and both assume much of their colors from the local aggregates (sand and gravel) used in their production, **15**, **16**.

Look very closely at both materials—a problem in determining their color is that the aggregates that are visible all vary slightly in color, but each is tiny in size. The overall effect is that concrete tends to be more buff or tan in color, where asphalt—as the oils leach away—goes toward gray, but often with other color highlights. On roadways, exposure to the sun and rain along with tire wear leaves the tread area a little lighter, while oil

**15**

Asphalt quickly loses its black coloration as the aggregate becomes visible. The color will vary between regions as the aggregate changes, so observation is important. There is a dark stain down the center of each lane from oil drippings, normally more pronounced in the more heavily travelled right lane. *CJ Riley*

This closeup view of a highway, with a joint between asphalt (left) and concrete, illustrates the differences in color, along with the varied color of small pieces of aggregate that make up the materials. *CJ Riley*

**16**

**17**

Dirt and gravel roads show variation in color, in this case from the tan dry areas to the much darker damp spots. *CJ Riley*

**18**

Although water is nominally clear, its reflective quality often makes it take on the coloring of its surroundings. Here, the blue sky and the green of the trees are part of this pond's coloring. *CJ Riley*

**19**

Trees are not uniform in color. Each species has its own shade and each season produces variations. Grasses and shrubs are similar. There are at least seven shades of green in this photo. *CJ Riley*

dripping down the center of the lanes leaves darker stains—the reverse of what is often modeled. So, start with lighter shades of the basic material and weather from there.

Dirt and gravel roads—along with gravel parking lots and railroad ballast—vary widely in color, and most are a mix of several colors. Note how the parking lot in **7** and the gravel road in **17** both include a wide range of colors from dark to light shades. This is a common mistake in modeling, when we grab a bag of "gray ballast" or "brown ballast" where every granule is the exact same color. These materials should have variation, even if it is subtle.

Another example is water: Water is not blue! Water seen up close is substantially clear, of course, but large bodies of water viewed from an angle or in the distance usually take on the color of the sky or immediate surroundings, **18**. This can mean bright blue on a sunny day, slate gray when cloudy, or green when reflecting overhanging trees. Depending on water depth and viewing angle, water can take on some of the colors of impurities. Red Creek in West Virginia has its headwaters in peat bogs, so the color (surprisc) is reddish, the color of weak tea. Creeks in mining areas are often polluted with mine drainage, staining everything a bright orange. Ponds may have an algae

bloom, giving them a green color. Rivers may carry a lot of silt, making them a muddy brown. Clear, shallow streams and bodies of water can allow seeing the bottoms, with rocks and other details.

There are dozens of ways to model water, and most can work well, depending on the desired effect. A slight amount of appropriate color added to a flat stream bottom or to the first couple of coats of resin before pouring will add realism. But final coats of "water" (resin, gloss medium, or other material) should be clear, since water is mostly clear. Study the real world before you begin to pour water.

Are trees green? The not-so-obvious answer is *sometimes*, **19**. Deciduous trees can be many shades of green, varying from almost lime green in early spring, through an olive green and then into fall colors. Trees with needles vary from primarily dark green to almost black, but some are quite yellow. They also seem darker in the snow. When modeling a forest, whether individual trees or a puff-ball canopy, clustering different shades of green with occasional clusters of evergreens produces a typical Appalachian forest. You will have to determine what is the right mix for your area, but the answer is *not* a uniform shade of green, except at great distances where the colors become hazy or muted.

**LEARNING POINTS** ➡

**1.** Perception of color changes with the type of light.

**2.** Use lighter colors in modeling to compensate for dimmer inside lighting.

**3.** Prototype paint colors chalk and fade over time.

**4.** Weathering affects colors.

**5.** Nature does not produce uniform colors.

**6.** Don't be afraid to change a color that looks wrong.

When modeling fall, keep in mind that trees normally clump together according to variety, so randomly mixing orange, yellow and red foliage doesn't look authentic. Different species change at different times, so a mixture of green, lightly tinged with color, and brightly colored trees is most realistic, along with a few brown-leafed and bare trees. Much of the commercially available foliage material is also quite bright, so I spray a rusty color lightly over my fall forests to tone down the brightness and blend the colors a bit. This is not to discourage you from placing that brilliant red maple in front of a white country church—that is a signature scene in many places.

# CHAPTER NINE

# Names and signs

Some of the most important decisions on a model railroad involve names: the name of the railroad itself, along with place names, industry names, and town names. If you are following a specific prototype, most of the naming will appropriately be taken from what you are modeling; when freelancing, naming choices become more critical to capturing the feeling of a real place, **1**.

Eric Brooman's HO scale Utah Belt is a freelanced layout set in the West. By basing his model railroad on a prototype (the Cotton Belt, or St. Louis Southwestern), he gave it a genuine flavor that is quite believable. *Eric Brooman*

1

The cities that gave their name to the Atchison, Topeka & Santa Fe—usually simply called the Santa Fe—were far more minor in significance to the railroad than its eventual end points of Chicago and Los Angeles. *Santa Fe*

The naming of towns and businesses is important to defining the setting and adding to the believability of a model railroad. When freelancing, the challenge of believability and the sense of rightness is even more difficult. Carefully chosen names can quickly provide the essence of a place and time well before the actual modeling can do so.

## Naming your railroad

Naming starts with the model railroad itself. Be careful here, for down this path lurks many dragons. It was once common to use puns or other cute names, clearly creating an image of toy trains. Moonlight & Violins, Bent Spaghetti Lines, and Hardscrabble & Great Divide were all well-known model railroads from the 1940s into the '60s. Even the legendary John Allen fell into that trap, much to his later regret, with his Gorre & Daphetid (the pun is "gory and defeated"). Although John admittedly grew tired

of the name, he felt trapped and never changed it. It is best to avoid those traps by choosing names rooted in the real world.

While modelers of a specific prototype railroad would seem to have this covered, even there difficulties can lurk. For example, one might choose to model the Baltimore & Ohio, but since the prototype's entire line from Baltimore to Chicago and St. Louis is not doable by even a large club, there must be a focus. That focus could be the main line up Sand Patch grade, the Georgetown branch, the area surrounding Cumberland, Md., a stretch of Indiana farm country, or perhaps street running on the Baltimore waterfront.

The home road equipment would be lettered B&O, and one would indeed be modeling the Baltimore & Ohio Railroad, but a name more descriptive of the area included might be chosen for the model railroad itself, such as "Baltimore & Ohio: Georgetown

Branch." Doing this makes it easy for others to quickly grasp what you're trying to accomplish.

On the other hand, freelancers who wish to choose a believable name need to be careful, lest they fall into the cutesy trap. Prototype railroads when newly chartered often chose grandiose names to gain the interest (and money) of investors. Many failed to reach at least one of their heralded terminal points—for example, the St. Louis-San Francisco, commonly known as the Frisco, was a major railroad (more than 5,000 route miles) that indeed served St. Louis but fell about 1,300 miles short of San Francisco.

On the other hand, more than a few railroads exceeded their namesake cities: the Atchison, Topeka & Santa Fe, **2**, named after three relatively small cities (albeit two state capitols) ultimately connected Los Angeles and Chicago. The mighty Pennsylvania Railroad and the New York Central, **3**, were two of the country's largest railroads, and likewise connected many more states and covered far more area than their names would indicate.

Along with cities, other common railroad name components include regions and directions (Lehigh Valley; Chicago & North Western; St. Louis Southwestern), lakes (Pittsburgh & Lake Erie; Denver & Salt Lake) or shores of lakes or oceans (Duluth, South Shore & Atlantic; Florida East Coast; Southern Pacific), rivers (Lehigh & Hudson River), states (Missouri Pacific; Texas & Pacific), route descriptions (Belt Railway of Chicago), corporate holding companies or organizations (Conrail for Consolidated Rail Corporation), or initials of merged rail lines (CSX, BNSF).

Nicknames can be part of the larger name (Santa Fe for Atchison, Topeka & Santa Fe; Burlington Route for Chicago, Burlington & Quincy) or can describe a region or area (Cotton Belt for St. Louis Southwestern), or something completely different (Nickel Plate Road for New York, Chicago & St. Louis).

The name New York Central implied a region of the named state, but it was actually a large railroad that spanned a far greater area—including through the very un-New York-like scenery near Goshen, Indiana. *Ira H. Eigsti*

The nature of your own railroad needs to be defined before a name is chosen. A wandering short line wouldn't likely be named for cities located 1,000 miles apart. New Hope & Ivyland has a name that is easily accepted as a short line (which it is, based in New Hope, Pa.), as does

Springfield Terminal.

Freelancing a major cross-country railroad name is much harder to do credibly, since the obvious names are already taken and well known, but it can be done. Regional names, however, are much easier. Allen McClelland's well-known HO layout, the Virginian

Allen McClelland named his HO railroad the Virginian & Ohio, a name sounding as if were steeped in the West Virginia coal mining traditions. The large V&O logo at right is the more contemporary "Appalachian Lines" scheme, a Chessie System-like amalgamation of his railroad with those of two friends. The middle loco is from Tony Koester's Allegheny Midland, another railroad in the system. *W. Allen McClelland*

**5**

I began modeling with the Beaver Forks & Muddgut, a shortline name. The name Mudgut was spotted on a hand-lettered sign pointing down a dirt road and the extra "d" was added whimsically. Beaver Forks was inspired by an early interest in the aquatic rodents that inspired my never-completed first book. The Brady Lumber Co. in the background was named for a noted logger in the '30s from the Gauley Valley. *CJ Riley*

& Ohio, **4**, is a good example as it clearly indicates its location. Eric Brooman's HO scale Utah Belt, based on the prototype Cotton Belt (St. Louis Southwestern) does likewise.

After much consideration and an unsatisfactory early experiment with Beaver Forks & Muddgut (an obvious shortline name), **5**, my own railroad became the Kanawha & Western Allegheny, combining a major river with a regional name in a north/

south line through the West Virginia coalfields (thus providing a reason for its existence).

I recommend avoiding grandiose names such as Atlantic & Pacific or Virginia & San Diego, since they imply a vast rail network that never existed in the real world. Historically most major eastern lines had western terminals at Chicago, St. Louis or New Orleans, with most western lines having their eastern terminals in those cities. If

modeling the current era, then most of the former transcontinental roads have disappeared through merger (not that they ever were truly transcontinental).

## Naming places

Friendships normally grow out of the hobby, so naming of towns and businesses after friends and family members is very logical and perhaps even necessary to smooth over "right-of-way" acquisition. It is all too easy to simply tack on "-burg" or "-ville" following a person's name. While that practice might have a prototypical basis, an abundance of Smithvilles, Christowns, or Marthaburgs on one layout will not ring true for most observers. Other suffixes that are most descriptive of place can help, such as Smith's Corners or Christopher Creek, but some names adapt quite easily to direct application. Thomas and Luke were towns on the Western Maryland and St. George was nearby. Last names are often used directly, such as Davis, Elkins, and Sutton, all in West Virginia. A little subtlety in the transfer of people's names goes a long way toward realism.

Of course, much of this problem disappears if modeling real locations. Looking at a map for the region or area being modeled will provide some good, realistic examples.

Railroads named every location of even minor importance, **6**. Whether it was a tower, siding switch, tunnel, road crossing, spur track, or bridge, it was named and/or numbered (usually based on milepost location). The "why" is obvious with a little thought. On timetables, stating the location (station name, even if there was no depot building) for meets or passes involving other trains was critically important for train order operation. If repairs were needed to a bridge, sending a crew to bridge 214.3 was definite; sending them to "the bridge where the railroad crosses the Deep River for the fourth time" isn't as accurate. Appropriate signs were provided, even at each end of remote sidings, to make the locations perfectly clear. There could be no misunderstanding without disastrous consequences.

**6**

This weather-beaten shelter proudly carrying the name CAMP APPALACHIA is an example of how naming every location along with prominent mile posts are important for operations on a railroad. *CJ Riley collection*

**7**

Early mileposts were often substantial signs, as with this concrete marker on the New York Central's Boston & Albany line. *CJ Riley collection*

Similarly, mileposts were commonly used as identification of location. Mileposts may be concrete, **7**, or cast iron on older lines, but in later times, simple small sheet-metal signs or narrow bands of paint, metal, or reflective tape were wrapped around line-side poles identifying miles and sometimes half and quarter miles, depending on the number of stripes. With the advent of radio communication, most signal and power lines along the tracks have been taken out of service, but the poles (or shortened versions) were often kept as mile indicators.

Railroads were fond of painting their names on bridges if the bridge was visible from nearby roads or traffic areas. The Western Maryland paralleled the B&O along much of their routes between Cumberland, Md., and Connellsville, Pa. There is a remote spot called Pinkerton where the

**8**

**Railroads often paint their names on the sides of bridges as free advertising as much as for identification. Here the Western Maryland bridge is visible to passengers on the parallel Baltimore & Ohio tracks so the name is on this side only.** *CJ Riley*

two lines are on the same side of the Youghiogheny River, just two hundred feet apart, and the Western Maryland proudly displayed its name on only

one side of its bridge—the side facing the passengers on B&O trains, **8**. The B&O did not find it necessary to paint its own name at that location. This is

## SIGNS AND TYPEFACES

Convincing signs require the same attention to prototype appearance as do other scenic details. The three most common errors in model signs are poor name choices (such as Ed's Steel Foundry, or other names not suggestive of the business in question); typeface choices which are not realistic on signs; and use of anachronistic typefaces. By far the most anachronistic are now-common faces such as Helvetica. These may be fine fonts in their own right but may not have been introduced at the time modeled.  For better choices, particularly in avoiding anachronism, a little typeface history is helpful, and there are many online resources that can be consulted. For the examples just given, Helvetica was released for commercial use in 1957. In the latter decades of the 20th century it became very widely used for signage and many governmental and industrial uses, but prior to about 1965 was little used for such purposes.

Even a superficial look at period photographs, such as the above view of Alexandria, Va., in 1940, will show that signs were dominated by sans-serif lettering. Notice the term "lettering" and not "typeface." It is still true today, and was a dominant fact before the 1970s, that most signs are painted by sign painters, not printed from type. Luckily there are many sign painter-styled typefaces available today, so this look can be achieved relatively easily in model signs with careful typeface choices.

The dominance of sans-serif signage does not exclude serif lettering, but the need for signs to be easily and promptly read

**This street view of Alexandria, La., in 1940, shows a wide variety of sign styles, but in looking at the graphics it is relatively easy to determine the era.** *Marion Post Wolcott, Library of Congress*

means that such lettering tends to be fairly bold and simple in design. Even company logos may have bolder lettering in signs than in, say, letterhead. Luckily, many suitable typefaces are available on the internet today for minimal prices or free. Once a general style has been chosen, one can readily find typefaces of that general character through sites such as Identifont (www.identifont.com).

For an elementary but very clear and concise introduction to this subject, there is nothing better than Robin Williams' books. The most introductory of her works is *The Non-designer's Type Book*, published by Peachpit Press and readily available on the internet.—*Tony Thompson*

**9**

The Kanawha's name is prominent on this bridge, again on one side only. As with the WM bridge in 8, there was no point in wasting effort by lettering the less visible side. *CJ Riley*

easy to duplicate on model bridges with decals or dry transfers, **9**.

Other items also often received a personal touch unique to a particular railroad, including signs—the Pennsylvania's keystone-shaped whistle posts are a prime example, **10**, or, as done by many railroads, including the name on crossbuck signs and NO TRESPASSING and other warning signs, **11**. You'll also often find railroad names or logos placed on various railroad buildings and equipment, **12**, **13**. Many of these are easy to capture in miniature.

## Business names

When it comes to business names— when a prototype isn't relevant— friends and family names can be accommodated realistically with a little extra care. First names are fine for small businesses, such as Sam's Market or Skip's Cafe, but first names generally don't work well for industrial situations. Sam's Steel Mill simply won't ring true. Industrial names are often regionally inspired, such as Algoma Steel, or represent mergers: Consolidation Coal (commonly called "Consol"). The name of the business often, but not always,

relates to the size of the business: United States Steel Corporation or the Corner Tavern.

I have made good use of regional names on my own railroad in order to help tie it into the real world, beginning with the railroad name itself: Kanawha & Western Allegheny (although with a little more care I would have realized that it would be spelled "Alleghany" as is common in its locale). Gauley Valley Feeds (fictional), **14**, in the town of Gauley Mills (real) and Elk River Transfer (fictional), **15**, in the town of Beaver Forks (fictional) use two of the area's major rivers in their names. Hemlock Mines, **16**, besides using the plural to imply additional sites, picks up on the tree species so important to the logging industry in West Virginia.

Those whose modeling is based in other parts of the country can likewise take advantage of regional names for businesses. For example, Cascade, Puget Sound (or just Puget), or Olympic (or Olympia) firmly attach a business to the Seattle area, even though the Cascade Mountains run down into Oregon. Hudson, Mohawk, and Big Apple are obviously New York based. Gulf, Palms, Beach and similar names carry one to the Southeast. All regions will have signature names that are instant identifiers, and you should be able to compile your own relevant lists.

I have not forgotten friends, nor have I ever been accused of not

**10**

Whistle posts installed appropriate distances from grade crossings alert the engineer to warn motorists. The Pennsylvania's keystone logo clearly identifies ownership. *CJ Riley*

**11**

Liability, safety, and security are always a concern, so NO TRESPASSING signs are prominent at most facilities, as well as bridges, right-of-way paths, tunnels, and other locations. *CJ Riley*

**12**

Equipment sheds are sometimes labeled with signs; the Chessie System decided this shed was worthy of a painted logo. *CJ Riley*

**13**

This wheelbarrow rated a Chessie logo within a logo. Details like this can be eye-catchers on a layout. *CJ Riley*

**14**

This feed mill is identified as to its locale along with the products sold. The sign has a border, almost a constant in older signs. After lettering was applied to thin styrene, the yellow from a hi-lighter provided some color. *CJ Riley*

**15**

Elk River Transfer is another local identifier. The lettering was done with decals, first with black and then offset in white, providing a shadow effect. In the rush to finish the model for a contest, I mangled the alignment and ran out of the appropriate letters. To distract the eye from this, a man on a ladder changing a light bulb saves the day. *CJ Riley*

**16**

Hemlock Mines refers to a common tree in West Virginia; Bergoo is a real town deep in the mountains. The weathering effects are as important as the name itself; I described how I created the sign and weathered it and the structure in Chapter 7. *CJ Riley*

having a sense of humor, so I have thus far picked on two friends for the names of small industries. One friend once confessed having longed for the nickname Ace as a youngster. From that moment, in appreciation of his electrical engineering Ph.D., he became known as the "electrical ace" so Ace Electrical Supplies was born. Another friend, a metallurgist with two rambunctious sons, inspired a nearby junk yard: A.W. Thompson & Sons, Demolition and Salvage. In both cases, visitors to the layout room who don't know the gentlemen involved accept the business names at face value, not feeling left out of a joke they don't quite understand.

Mountaineer Brewing Co. (a regional name) is prominent on my brewery, along with the brand name Old Bulldog Beer, **17**, reflecting a

**17**

Having always raised bulldogs, I was glad to be able to create a beer brand using the image. Old Bulldog Beer is a product of the Mountaineer Brewing Co., and the mountaineer is a symbol of West Virginia. The bulldog was hand drawn and added to the sign, lettered with dry transfers, then hand-colored. *CJ Riley*

18

This Western Auto roof sign is an iconic image that shows up in the background of many photos of Kansas City. Including such a signature sign enhances the credibility and sense of rightness of a model of that area. *Nicholas Muff*

long series of family pets. I left off the slogan, "It's the Water" to avoid fuzzy tongues on my beer-drinking friends, but the sign includes a founding date to establish a sense of passing time and anchor the building in a real place and time.

There is a long tradition in the hobby of naming businesses or industries with puns or other amusing names. I have no quarrel with this, but many modelers have discovered that puns and cute names often grow tiresome over time.

As a final source, look to the prototype for inspiration—even if you're freelancing. Maps, old Yellow Pages from the area and era (check eBay), business directories, period photographs (and books), and similar sources are valuable. If the area you model is far from home, local libraries, local historical societies, and the internet can be a big help.

I was especially fortunate to have found a wonderful book at the Cass Scenic Railroad's company store titled *Gauley Mountain,* by Louise McNeill. It contains the history of the Gauley region, in poetry form, from the first white settler, named Dan O'Kane, through the CCC reforestation programs in the 1930s. The book is a treasure, containing a great many names and the occupations that go with them, all authentic to the area I am modeling. A trip through the region revealed many of the same names still used on businesses at that time. It was a simple matter to adapt these names on my layout.

Claudius Crozet, Napoleon's engineer and builder of tunnels for

19

The big yellow Lee Overalls sign behind Chicago's Dearborn Station (above left, to the left of the station's clock tower) is an iconic symbol that shows up in many photos of the station. *Louis A. Marre collection*

20

Every region has its tourist attractions that advertise along the highway. A common one in eastern Tennessee is Rock City, near Chattanooga. *CJ Riley*

21

Once more common but still seen, these hand-painted Mail Pouch Tobacco advertisements were done, with the agreement of the farmers, by traveling sign painters who adjusted the image to the shape and size of the wall facing the road. *CJ Riley*

the Chesapeake & Ohio, built the first wagon road into the Gauley region and I named the Kanawha's doodlebug for him. Sol Brady was an early logger, so the lumber company in Gauley Mills became the Brady Lumber Co. The yard building's sign identifies two locations—Gauley Mills (modeled) and Webster Springs, a more prominent (but not modeled) town in the region, thus reinforcing the "beyond-the-basement" concept.

## Signs help define era and location

Since railroad equipment might have a life span of 40 years or so, and structures even longer, it is difficult for those items alone to define a desired era. Highway vehicles are probably the most recognizable era-definers to most viewers, but more subtle items such as clothing styles, highway signs, structure signs, and other details can further set the mood and period being modeled. If your intention is to represent a specific time and place, then extra care taken here will pay dividends when visitors arrive.

If modeling a specific prototype area, there may be signature signs that clearly identify the location. Two well-known examples from older periods are the large roof-mounted Western Auto sign that dominated the skyline behind Kansas City Union Station, **18**, and a Lee Work Clothes sign painted on a building side that loomed over

Chicago's Dearborn Station, **19**.

The signs you need may not be as prominent as these, but inclusion of a signature sign is a sure-fire identifier. When freelancing, you might have a broader choice of potential signs, but keep to what would be typical or even a variation of a typical sign in your modeled area. "See Rock City," **20**, and "See Ruby Falls" are common along highways in the Chattanooga region, as are Mail Pouch Tobacco signs, **21**, painted on barns in many regions, particularly in Appalachia.

Once appropriate names have been chosen, they must be applied to structures and sign boards. It is important to use a variety of fonts and styles on signs, as well as different methods of construction, to avoid the appearance that they were all painted and installed at the same time by the same sign painter.

Modelers today have many options for making realistic signs, including many styles of alphabet decals and dry transfers, commercial ready-made sign graphics on paper and as decals, and three-dimensional signs as plastic and laser-cut wood kits. Computer graphics and photo-editing software are readily available—along with digital cameras—for making your own designs, re-creating real signs, or modifying existing signs. You can carefully photograph a sign (or even the entire side of a building), with flaws and weathering included, and manipulate it

**Here's an excellent example of a prototype sign, professionally rendered. The name of the coal company is the largest lettering; the mine identification and location are smaller. The sign maker, McNally-Pittsburgh, is identified separately.**
*CJ Riley collection*

digitally to be used on a model.

Proper typefaces, lettering styles, and sign designs are very important in establishing a sense of time and place, **22**. Examination of the backgrounds in railroad photographs can help you understand what is (and was) typical. It's too easy to fall into the trap, often seen in photos of layouts, of signs plastered all over buildings with little concern as to era compatibility or what would actually be done if it were a real scene.

The wrong lettering style can kill the effect of a scene—for example, modern typefaces such as Helvetica (first developed in 1957) look out of place on a steam-era layout. Doing a little research on typefaces or fonts will be of great benefit (see the sidebar on page 81 for further detail). Typefaces and signs that are older than the era being modeled can work, but must be weathered and positioned to reflect their apparent age.

A common type of sign through multiple eras, from the early 1900s to the present, are large signs painted on the sides of multistory masonry buildings identifying the owner and/or the products provided, **23**, **24**, **25**. The lettering styles have evolved over time, but the basic style of most is a black background with white lettering and a white border. Color is occasionally added for emphasis, but a sign without a border is uncommon.

Study photos and look for older buildings when traveling in order to capture the proper appearance of these signs. If you're freelancing, it's difficult to go wrong with using this white/black/border combo. It is a subtle but important component to your sense of rightness. Also consider "ghost signs," those older signs painted onto buildings long ago that are slowly fading and peeling away, **26**. This is a

**Many older buildings have large signs painted on their blank walls, but such large signs have been prohibited in many places by sign ordinances since in the 1960s. Note the black background and the blue border that frames the image, and the painter's logo in the lower right-hand corner.** *CJ Riley*

**When windows are present, the sign must be adapted to the window pattern. This well-weathered sign was obviously renewed down toward the bottom.** *CJ Riley*

**25**

The C.S. Willis feed mill is blessed with a plethora of signs on all sides. One is faded away and partly painted over; the Reading Anthracite sign seems new, probably because it was porcelain enamel on steel. The checkerboard pattern is a standard with Purina. *CJ Riley collection*

**26**

"Ghost" signs add a lot of character to otherwise blank walls. There are several sources of ghost sign decals and dry transfers, but it is possible to photograph such a sign, adapt it in Photoshop, and apply it directly to a wall with all the weathering, texture and flaws included. *CJ Riley*

**27**

Paul Dolkos found some internet images of billboards appropriate for his November 1952 setting: an Eisenhower election ad and one for a 1953 model automobile being pasted over the previous year's poster. There can be little doubt as to when this scene is happening. *Paul Dolkos*

## LEARNING POINTS ➜

**1.** Select a realistic railroad name you can live with for the long term.

**2.** Avoid pun or joke layout or business names, as even the best puns can quickly become stale.

**3.** Use regional names for places and businesses.

**4.** Choose appropriate lettering styles, sign styles, and artwork for the era modeled.

**5.** Use a wide variety of homemade and commercial graphics for variety.

legitimate excuse to have otherwise inappropriately old signage in a more modern era.

Billboards are another attention-grabber, and since they are generally kept up to date, they are effective at establishing a particular era, season, and locale, **27**. A billboard advertising recently introduced car models or with a Thanksgiving or Christmas theme would enhance an autumn scene. Likewise, billboards advertising local businesses or institutions will help cement the locale. Billboards are typically changed on a regular basis, so a common modeling mistake is a sign advertising a long-discontinued brand of soap in a more modern era, or a modern cola logo in an older one.

With a little care and planning, signs can be a major force in projecting the desired image of a model railroad.

Some thought given to the selection of names and consideration of the appropriate construction methods will help make the finished scene appear to be a small slice of the real world.

1

CHAPTER TEN

# Setting the mood

**Atmosphere of one kind is this hazy shot of the diesel shops on Allen McClelland's HO scale Virginian & Ohio. But atmosphere can have many other important meanings as well.**
*W. Allen McClelland*

While creating a mood on the model railroad should be our main focus, **1**, much can be done with the railroad room or basement and environs to add aura, mystique, and a sense of place and era. Creating a meaningful environment can supplement all of our other efforts in producing an understanding of the time and place we are presenting. While basement railroad rooms are common, other rooms are frequently used and these comments apply to any chosen location.

**2**

**3**

J.J. Johnson had an artist paint the walls between his layout and workshop/guest room in this fanciful log cabin theme. The raccoon visible outside the room can be seen peering through the window on the inside, while his friend is on the ceiling, peering through the damaged roof. *CJ Riley*

I built this three-quarter-size boxcar wall at the entrance to my train room using tongue-and-groove "porch flooring" for the wall, hardboard for metal reinforcing straps, and carriage bolt heads as rivets. The wood was pre-weathered using modeling techniques and the lettering applied using stencils and paint. *CJ Riley*

Begin with the approach to your room. I have seen a train room off a home's main living space that was painted (by a professional) with a mural of an exterior depot wall. A nearby wall around the work room/ spare bedroom was painted as a log cabin, complete with raccoon peering in the window, **2**. On the opposite face of that wall was the same scene from the interior perspective.

It is certainly not necessary to go that far, as charming as that might sound, but much can be done to ease the transition from living space to a

working railroad set in your chosen era. The walls of the basement stairs would ideally be finished and can be decorated with appropriate railroad memorabilia. In my former home, I built a wall at the bottom of the stairs with a pocket door to keep pets away from the trains. The wall was finished to look like the left-hand portion of an older double sheathed wooden boxcar side, complete with my model railroad's reporting marks, chalk marks and some historical graffiti, **3**. I found an old grab iron buried in the cinders while waiting for a steam excursion to exit Sand

Patch tunnel on the Baltimore & Ohio and mounted it appropriately.

Once in the layout room, work and operating sessions are enhanced if the room is finished and well lighted. Room finishing and decor doesn't need to be fancy or expensive, but the more "railroady" the better. My own preference is to separate the railroad from the aisles with a finished fascia and lighting valance. With minimal lighting in the aisles, the railroad is framed and enhanced like the stage in a theater. It also helps to have an assigned sitting/congregating area

# Chessie's Hero!

OUR THOUGHTS, like those of Chessie, are on those far away. We're dreaming of the time when the heroic men and women now serving this nation will be home again, devoting their lives to pleasant pursuits of living.

That's why folks of the Chesapeake and Ohio are doing everything in their power to speed the

accommodations we were once able to provide.

But, when the job is all over, the railroads will again give you the safest, most comfortable, most enjoyable transportation your travel dollar can buy.

The illustration above is from the new 1945 Chessie calendar. We're not having many calen-

**4**

Framed period advertisements, such as this World War II era "Chessie Goes to War" magazine ad, reinforce the era.

5

An inexpensive battery-operated clock combined with a sheet styrene ring with strip styrene trim provides railroad atmosphere. The paint and lettering style match those on the railroad fascia. *CJ Riley*

6

The highlight of Dr. Nicholas Muff's layout room is the cab portion of an F7 diesel rescued from a scrap yard, restored, and painted in the colors used on the Kansas City Southern's *Southern Belle*. This artifact was lowered into the basement addition before the house above was framed. *Nicholas Muff*

for crews and visitors. This removes considerable chatter from the railroad area that can detract from the intended feeling of a working railroad. Some comfortable seating, reading material, snacks, and railroadiana will complete a comfortable crew area.

Other enhancements can include era-appropriate music, as well as calendars and images on the walls relative to the era modeled. My own railroad is set during World War II so I have big band music playing in the background, and the walls feature mounted framed ads from period magazines, including a group of the Chesapeake & Ohio's "Chessie goes to

War" series on the walls, 4, along with an appropriate calendar from October 1942. I also created a railroad wall clock using an inexpensive, modern battery-powered clock to which I added a styrene ring with my free-lanced railroad's name on it, 5.

Among the most impressive layout settings belongs to Dr. Nicholas Muff, a Kansas City Southern fan who models the area around Kansas City Union Terminal with an almost religious attention to the

prototype. His railroad is in a specially constructed basement addition that includes a genuine, full-size Electro-Motive F7 cab painted in the KCS scheme of the 1950s, 6, 7. The unit, from the rear cab wall to the nose, was lowered in place before the house above was framed. When the door to the cab's engine room is opened, the space is filled with a life-size photo of the locomotive's former engine room taken through the door. The cab features an amped-up sound unit and

7

The F7's cab interior is restored, and viewers can sit on the fireman's or engineer's seats and view the model railroad. *Nicholas Muff*

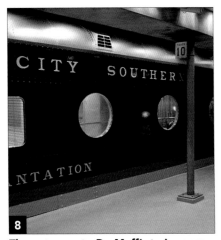

**8**

The entrance to Dr. Muff's train room is through a re-creation of a Kansas City Southern passenger car, fitted out as a guest room with era-appropriate magazines and newspapers and many carefully chosen details to help set the atmosphere. *Nicholas Muff*

**9**

Fascias and valances help frame and emphasize the railroad. I used gloss black paint on Masonite hardboard for the valance with a Norfolk & Western inspired tuscan red band where town names are applied. The matching fascia has recessed panels to protect switches. *CJ Riley*

**10**

Computer-generated signs are easy to make and add to the fascia or valance. The important information is all here. *W. Allen McClelland*

the air horns work—a great surprise to visitors.

The steps descending to Dr. Muff's basement have walls finished to represent Kansas City Union Terminal. They lead to the end wall at the bottom—and a mural of the station platform painted in perspective. Adjacent is a partial re-creation of a KCS lightweight passenger car, **8**, framed in wood and Masonite with appropriate salvaged plumbing fittings, seats, berths, china, and tableware. The train room entrance is through the car, which functions as a guest room as well. Dr. Muff is fond of wearing his KCS conductor's uniform while giving tours.

I understand that some of these efforts may be perceived as extreme— many modelers simply don't have the available space or funds to furnish a basement or railroad room to this extent. The point here is to provide ideas and show what's possible, and encourage you to make your railroad room at least as attractive as the layout itself and to reinforce the mood and image for which you are striving.

Bare concrete floors, block walls, and exposed ceiling joists, ductwork, and plumbing are unnecessary visual distractions and contribute dirt and dust to the room. Framing the walls and adding insulation and drywall will

not only improve the appearance: It will make the unfinished space warmer. A finished ceiling (either suspended panels and framing or simply drywall), will make the area brighter and and eliminate falling dust. All of this should be done before starting benchwork.

For concrete floors, since concrete dust is very abrasive, it is wise at minimum to paint the concrete with an appropriate floor paint/sealer. Carpeting is easier on the feet and can deaden sound. Carpet squares are a simple do-it-yourself project and could be confined to the aisles to save money; another option is interlocking rubber floor tiles. All of these improvements will make your layout room a more welcoming, inviting area that you'll want to spend more time in.

For the layout, fascias (the front-facing panels around the edges of the benchwork) and valances (vertical panels hanging from the ceiling that follow the edge of the benchwork and screen above-layout lighting) can be made from various materials and finishes, depending on personal taste, **9**. Wood paneling was quite popular for a period into the 1980s, but I don't recommend it: In most cases it calls attention to itself and away from the railroad. Tempered hardboard (such as Masonite) works well as it is easily

cut, curved, mounted, and painted. Large styrene sheets can be purchased from commercial plastic suppliers. This material is also flexible, easy to cut, and provides a smooth, even surface (be sure the paint you use will work well on plastic).

Much has been written about the best color for painting the fascia and valance, a decision that is not always obvious but is very personal. The rear of the lighting valance should be white to maximize light reflection above the layout. On the aisle side, many choose to paint the fascia and valance to match the scenery, such as a sandy tan for a desert theme or dark green for an Appalachian railroad. Some choose to use their railroad's primary color:

**Labeling locations of streets, rivers, and other significant points on the fascia will assist visiting operators. Tom Johnson also continues scenic materials on the fascia on his HO layout.** *Tom Johnson*

Tuscan red for a Pennsy layout, for example.

However, I prefer black. It is the color most used in stage productions to frame scenes and hide distractions. It is the color of steam locos if modeling that era. But mostly, it provides a very strong frame, leaving the brightly lit railroad glowing in an otherwise darkened room, just like the set in a stage play.

The fascia and/or valance is also the most useful place to apply important information, such as the map direction, names of towns, streams, highways, track numbers in yards, or any other useful details that can assist modelers and viewers, **10**, **11**. Prototype photos of scenes modeled or even contest awards could be displayed on the fascia near the models.

Walls in the layout room can include any number of railroad-related items. Railroad advertising artwork was mentioned earlier; other possibilities include a prototype-style chalk board, **12**, for assigning operating jobs, a large map of the modeled area (or a system map of the prototype railroad if appropriate), railroad heralds or logos, locomotive builder's plates, display cases for special models or collectables—the list goes on. Use your imagination and rely on things that interest you or have special meaning for you.

## TRAIN NAMES

Railroad workers have many nicknames for trains, but these nicknames didn't always match official designations. Railroads' crack passenger trains were commonly named for marketing purposes and those names, such as *Broadway Limited*, *Denver Zephyr*, and *Super Chief*, are well known. Many priority freight trains were also named, often including either the initials or full names of terminal cities: GN's *Seattle Fast Freight*; or by service description, such as SP's *Overnight* merchandise train or the Baltimore & Ohio's *Southwest Steel Special*. Some were more colorful, such as the Alphabet Route's (NKP, W&LE, P&WV, WM, Reading, CNJ, L&HR, NYNH&H) *Alpha Jets*, IC's *Pork Chop*, and New Haven/PRR *Speed Witch*.

Peddler freights and local passenger trains were usually unnamed, but often blessed with unofficial and colorful monickers by railroaders. Prototype examples include the "Dirty Shirt," "Night Owl," "Bulldog," "Black Duck," "Candy Run," "Dive Bomber," "Mae West," "Rambler", and "Digger," to name just a few. Including such names in operating sessions adds much to the cultural authenticity of your railroad. A search of the internet will turn up hundreds of such examples. And if you can have a professional railroader operate or visit your layout, listen carefully to what he says.

Will your railroad operate with a dispatcher, have a Centralized Traffic Control (CTC) or similar signaling system, or have operators simulating local operator or tower operator positions? If so, having an office or

**12**

Small-town depots often had chalkboards for train information. You can make one using chalkboard paint; these can be useful for marking up jobs at an operating session. *CJ Riley*

**13**

Re-creating the atmosphere of an authentic dispatcher's or operator's office can be rewarding. This is the Chicago & North Western's North Proviso (Chicago) yardmaster's office during World War II. Note the clock and the plethora of notices, calendars, and other ephemera, as well as the heavy use of "bead board" on the walls and ceilings and the clock. *Library of Congress*

working area that captures the flavor of the real thing, **13**, will amplify the feeling that your model railroad has a place in the real world.

Ideally, a dispatcher will operate away from the trains, keeping the noise and chatter down. A dispatcher's "office" (which could be as simple as an alcove or a space under the basement stairs) should reflect the real thing, **14**. Most of us won't have the level of interest that inspires us to learn

Morse code, but simple things like having a basic phone system with a dispatcher's desk with a telescoping phone mouthpiece separate from the phone body add to realism. Clipboards,

a prototypical dispatchers board, a desk to have a train sheet, a period desk lamp, clock, train order pads and forms, and other visual items add much to capturing a dispatcher's experience.

## PROTOTYPE FLAVOR

My old office overlooked the former Pennsylvania Railroad Panhandle Bridge approach in downtown Pittsburgh. After Pennsy no longer used it, the bridge was appropriated by the local transit agency for light-rail use, rendering much of the trackage and associated railroad installations redundant, to be scrapped. I noticed that many of the Pennsy's unique cast stanchions for pipe railings—a signature item—were left in a pile for later disposal. While some would call it theft, my job with the city included historic preservation, so I chose to call it that. I never had an opportunity to use the pieces, so when I moved to the Pacific Northwest, I donated the pieces to a local Pennsy modeler who used them on a duck-under, adding genuine atmosphere to his PRR railroad room.

The Pennsylvania Railroad used cast iron stanchions with common iron pipe in railings across the system. Dr. Neal Schorr models this railing style on his O scale Pennsy railroad (left) as well as using the real thing (salvaged) to protect his stair pit duck-under (right). *Two photos: Neil Schorr*

14

A modeled dispatchers board, such as this one at Otis McGee's model railroad, adds both authentic atmosphere and operational realism. Boards like this have been built by many modelers, using both salvaged components and reproductions. *CJ Riley*

The important thing is to think of the entire railroad room as a setting that can enhance the images and mood you are trying to convey to both yourself and visitors. Care here will pay dividends in your model railroading experience.

## The "culture" of your railroad

While the railroad setting is important to creating a mood, you should also think about the little things relating to your prototype both on and off your layout, **14**. Figures are a key: Do you have Hispanic and African-American figures in percentages as appropriate for your era and region? If the era is appropriate, does your southern layout have Jim Crow segregated facilities? Including things on your layout that although considered offensive today are historically accurate should not be considered improper and might very well serve an educational function.

Because I model the fall of 1942, I have included many figures of soldiers, a draft board office, recruiting posters, Blue Star flags hanging in windows, presidential election posters, and a scrap drive. If modeling the 1950s, a disc jockey in a storefront or groups of musicians harmonizing on a street corner would add a strong sense of

time and a new "Blue Star Highway" sign would add history.

The modern world has what many consider a graffiti problem and modelers of these times should not avoid this prominent feature of railroads and their immediate environs. Many companies offer graffiti decal sets, and you could make your own by printing digital photos on blank or white decal paper with a home printer, or apply graffiti directly with paint markers or gel pens. Once again, it may be thought of as offensive, but it is part of modern life and I think it needs to be included for a layout of today to have a sense of "rightness."

It is also advantageous to increase realism by studying more subtle aspects of a culture. My Kanawha & Western Allegh*e*ny RR would be subtly improved if I had spelled it Allegh*a*ny, the common spelling in the area modeled. Likewise, Greenbri*a*r is regionally spelled Greenbri*e*r and I could easily discover other place spelling variations with some research.

Pronunciation can also be intensely local. I was once traveling through central West Virginia listening to a local talk show on the radio. A discussion began about the correct pronunciation of Kanawha, a county

and river in that area (and the source of my railroad name). The question was whether it should be 3 syllables or 2: Kan-AH-waw or Kan-AW. A gentleman called in claiming to be a professor of linguistics who had been born in the county. He forcefully insisted that it was pronounced with 3 syllables: "Kan-AW!" As in many regions, the natives may hear syllables (or letters) that outsiders don't, and sometimes add them where they don't appear.

I once met an Ohio modeler who included western Pennsylvania's Youghiogheny (Yok-uh-gay-nee) River in his railroad name. Unfortunately, he had been pronouncing it Yoff-ee-AH-guh-ney causing considerable confusion with some and jocularity among others. He was gently corrected.

There are similar variations in other areas. The pronunciation of the Cayuhoga River in Cleveland is debated, even among locals. Sequim Washington is pronounced Skwim, and Native American names such as Humptulips, Dosewallips and Lilliwaup enrich the language of the Salish Sea (Puget Sound). The Purgatoire River in Southeastern Colorado is also known as the Purgatory or Picketwire, (corruptions of the original) in some locales. Such variations exist around the country and one would be wise to listen carefully to help maintain authenticity.

The lesson? Learn about and pay attention to localisms. Learn from the protype.

### LEARNING POINTS →

**1.** Study localisms and, if possible, listen to area railroaders for more authenticity.

**2.** Think about iconic images that help define an era or location.

**3.** Make the railroad room and its approaches comfortable and "railroady" for atmosphere.

**4.** Don't be afraid to include cultural or historic details that may be offensive to some but are a part of history and thus, reality.

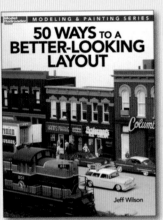
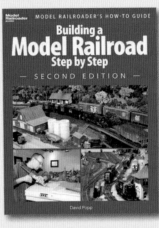
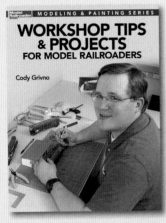
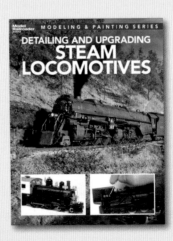